Cyberspace Solarium Comm

2021 Annual Report on Impler

August 2021

I0018066

The United States has a problem in cyberspace. the recent torrent of hacks, intrusions, breaches, ransomware, and shutdowns demonstrates that we have much more to do to secure Americans' lives and livelihoods online. This is true for the private sector, where it is far past time for business leaders to proactively protect critical infrastructure and secure sensitive information. It is also true for the government, where issues of jurisdiction, bureaucracy, and underinvestment hamper eorts to combat cyber threats, build effective public-private collaboration, and promote responsible behavior in cyberspace. Complex and interwoven challenges like these were precisely what motivated the Cyberspace Solarium Commission's work and informed the Commission's March 2020 report. Last year we concluded that attaining meaningful security in cyberspace requires action across many coordinated fronts. We have seen a great deal of progress in implementing the original 82 recommendations from that report, as well as the recommendations we added in white papers along the way.

This report explores the progress of the Cyberspace Solarium Commission. It is published as a convenience to those who may wish to have a quality professionally printed copy of the manual.

Should you have suggestions or feedback on ways to improve this book please send email to Books@OcotilloPress.com

---

Edited 2021 Ocotillo Press
ISBN 978-1-954285-80-4

Ocotillo Press
Houston, TX 77017
Books@OcotilloPress.com

CONTENTS

EXECUTIVE SUMMARY

The United States has a problem in cyberspace. The recent torrent of hacks, intrusions, breaches, ransomware, and shutdowns demonstrates that we have much more to do to secure Americans' lives and livelihoods online. This is true for the private sector, where it is far past time for business leaders to proactively protect critical infrastructure and secure sensitive information. It is also true for the government, where issues of jurisdiction, bureaucracy, and underinvestment hamper efforts to combat cyber threats, build effective public-private collaboration, and promote responsible behavior in cyberspace. Complex and interwoven challenges like these were precisely what motivated the Cyberspace Solarium Commission's work and informed the Commission's March 2020 report. Last year we concluded that attaining meaningful security in cyberspace requires action across many coordinated fronts. We have seen a great deal of progress in implementing the original 82 recommendations from that report, as well as the recommendations we added in white papers along the way.

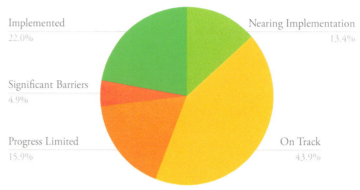

Progress of Solarium Report Recommendations

Implemented 22.0%

Nearing Implementation 13.4%

Significant Barriers 4.9%

Progress Limited 15.9%

On Track 43.9%

But these changes are just beginning, and the threat remains every bit as real this year. As a country, we all—businesses, government, civil society, and individuals—need to act with more speed and agility when it comes to securing cyberspace. That means investing in enterprise cybersecurity *before* attacks happen, developing a clear cyber strategy, sharing threat information at the speed of data, ensuring that our teachers have the tools they need to kindle a spark of interest that will one day lead a student to a cyber job, and so much more. Keeping in mind the monumental work still ahead of us, we find several highlights in assessing the Commission's progress to date:

Evaluating the Big Picture – The Commission's report was more than a collection of recommendations. It was also a strategic approach to and assessment of the cyber threat landscape. In some cases, the accuracy of the Commission's analysis is obvious: the drumbeat of significant cyberattacks undeniably increased as expected, but we certainly did not predict that the COVID-19 pandemic would create a new opportunity for such attacks. In other cases, evaluating the Commission's work is more difficult. While the Commission's strategic approach of layered cyber deterrence has remained a valuable framework for evaluating possible U.S. actions to defend against attacks of significant consequence, understanding its larger impact will require more time and better mechanisms for measuring improvements in national cybersecurity. In the meantime, individual recommendations that anchor that strategic approach are well on their way to implementation.

Major Steps Forward – A number of the Commission's key recommendations have been implemented by the Congress or executive branch; in other cases, significant progress toward their implementation is being made. The establishment, nomination, and confirmation of a **National Cyber Director** (Recommendation 1.3) represents significant progress toward implementing the Commission's highest-priority goals. The FY21 National Defense Authorization Act included provisions to **strengthen the Cybersecurity and Infrastructure Security Agency** (Recommendation 1.4), codify **Sector Risk Management Agencies** (Recommendation 3.1), establish a **Continuity of the Economy** plan (Recommendation 3.2), establish a **Joint Cyber Planning Office** (Recommendation 5.4), and require a **force structure assessment of the Cyber Mission Force** (Recommendation 6.1). Meanwhile, both Trump and Biden administration actions have made inroads toward implementing an information and communications technology or **ICT industrial base strategy** (Recommendation 4.6), and the President's Budget Request proposes a **Cyber Response and Recovery Fund** (Recommendation 3.3).

Remaining Priorities – Progress in implementing Commission recommendations has been remarkable, but not universal, and many key issues remain priorities for the Commission's future work. Codifying the concept of **Systemically Important Critical Infrastructure** (Recommendation 5.1) and establishing a **Joint Collaborative Environment** (Recommendation 5.2) continue to be complex, challenging, and high-priority goals. The **Cyber Diplomacy Act** (Recommendation 2.1), which has yet to pass the Senate, would implement the Commission's recommendation for a cyber-focused bureau at the State Department. Several recommendations—like the establishment of **House Permanent Select and Senate Select Committees on Cybersecurity** (Recommendation 1.2) and a **National Data Security and Privacy Protection Law** (Recommendation 4.7)—have met resistance and are unlikely to move forward in the near future. However, the Commission remains dedicated to refining and advancing these recommendations. The policy community may not be prepared to take on these hard problems today, but we are making sure that the recommendations are ready when the time comes.

The Commission is proud of its progress but recognizes that in order to determine where we go next in cybersecurity, we must be clear-eyed about what is not working. And we understand that many of the remaining recommendations are not low-hanging fruit; we need to keep climbing to get many of them done. Many critical recommendations are not implemented *yet*, but that does not mean we intend to write them off as a loss and move on. With that in mind, the analysis below does more than just enumerate recommendations that have or have not been implemented. It also outlines remaining priorities and the adaptations made by the Commission to improve its approach.

We have endeavored to be very careful in our use of the word "success" in this report. Real success is protecting national critical infrastructure from malicious cyber activity. We believe that these recommendations will help the country achieve that success, but we are under no illusions that the work ends when a recommendation becomes law or an executive order incorporates a Commission priority. This report draws a map connecting our current reality in cyberspace to a future when Americans can rely on the digital infrastructure that surrounds us. Implementation of the Commission's recommendations is only the very first step toward a connected world we can trust. All of us—and each of you—share responsibility for every step after that.

Senator Angus King (I-Maine)
Co-Chairman
Cyberspace Solarium Commission

Representative Mike Gallagher (R-Wisconsin)
Co-Chairman
Cyberspace Solarium Commission

COMMISSION BACKGROUND

The digital connectivity that has brought economic growth, technological dominance, and an improved quality of life to nearly every American has also created a strategic dilemma. The United States now operates in a cyber landscape that requires a level of data security, resilience, and trustworthiness that neither the U.S. government nor the private sector alone is currently equipped to provide. Moreover, shortfalls in agility, technical expertise, and unity of effort, both within the U.S. government and between the public and private sectors, are growing. For more than 20 years, nation-states and non-state actors have leveraged cyberspace to subvert American power, American security, and the American way of life. The perpetrators of these cyberattacks exploited weaknesses in both systems and strategy and assessed that their forays damaged the United States without triggering any significant retaliation. American restraint was met with unchecked predation.[1] The U.S. Cyberspace Solarium Commission (CSC) was established in the John S. McCain National Defense Authorization Act for Fiscal Year 2019 to address these challenges and "develop a consensus on a strategic approach to defending the United States in cyberspace against cyber attacks of significant consequences."[2]

To meet its mandate, the CSC produced a final report, published in March 2020, outlining a strategic approach and 82 recommendations for the U.S. government. In developing the final report, task forces met with more than 300 stakeholders from industry; academia; federal, state, and local governments; international organizations; and think tanks, and they stress-tested their recommendations through a series of red team reviews and a scenario-based Solarium event. Following the Solarium event, the Commissioners assessed each strategy and its supporting policy recommendations, providing formal feedback. The staff tabulated this feedback and used the insights and guidance to further refine the recommendations.

In the months following the launch of the final report, Commissioners and staff produced legislative proposals (where appropriate) to support its recommendations, and worked with relevant committees in the House and Senate to implement many of the Commission's original recommendations. In addition, the Commission issued four white papers with new and updated recommendations: they addressed lessons on cybersecurity from the pandemic, details on the national cyber director recommendation, a framework for a cybersecurity workforce development strategy, and proposals on how to secure America's information and communications technology (ICT) supply chains. A fifth white paper, published in January 2021, highlighted specific priorities for the incoming Biden-Harris administration. Many of the Commission's key recommendations have been enacted in legislation, but there is still more work to be done to meet the urgent challenges facing our nation, and much can be achieved through coordinated and thoughtful executive action.

This assessment is intended to review the implementation of the recommendations made by the Commission over the course of the previous year. The recommendations themselves are discussed in more detail in the Commission's final report and accompanying white papers.[3]

---

1   David Alexander, "Hagel, Ahead of China Trip, Urges Military Restraint in Cyberspace," *Reuters*, March 28, 2014, https://www.reuters.com/article/us-usa-defense-cybersecurity/hagel-ahead-of-china-trip-urges-military-restraint-in-cyberspace-idUSBREA2R1ZH20140328.

2   John S. McCain National Defense Authorization Act for Fiscal Year 2019, Pub. L. No. 115-232 [hereafter FY19 NDAA], § 1652, 132 Stat. 1636, 2140 (2018), https://www.govinfo.gov/content/pkg/PLAW-115publ232/pdf/PLAW-115publ232.pdf.

3   These publications are available at the Cyberspace Solarium Commission's website, www.solarium.gov.

EVALUATING PROGRESS

n many respects, the recommendations enumerated in the Cyberspace Solarium Commission's report and ensuing white papers are the most concrete basis on which to evaluate the Commission's progress. However, these recommendations are based on conclusions that the Commission reached during the deliberative process, and on the larger strategic framework implied by those conclusions. That is to say, the retrospective accuracy of the Commission's assumptions about the opportunities and threats in cyberspace must be part of an overall review of the Commission's work. Similarly, meaningful evaluation must also consider the Commission's strategic approach to addressing those opportunities and deterring threats. Accordingly, this section examines fundamental assumptions around what success looks like, the issues the Commission sought to address, and the strategic framework laid out in the Commission's March 2020 report. The section then establishes the methodology used in evaluating individual recommendations.

MEASURING IMPACT AND PROMOTING FUTURE SUCCESS

A secure cyberspace will never be a single, static goal. Making lasting progress toward improved cybersecurity is certain to be an ongoing, iterative process requiring the engagement of leaders across government, the private sector, civil society, and the international community of U.S. allies and partners. The implementation of CSC recommendations in law or policy must be seen only as the beginning of work toward a more stable, secure cyberspace. Accordingly, this report distinguishes between the implementation of a recommendation and the achievement of lasting success. Moreover, success of the Commission's overall strategy of layered cyber deterrence could be defined as its adoption through a national cyber strategy or, borrowing from the Commission's original mandate, "defending the United States in cyberspace against cyber attacks of significant consequences." Since, as a practical matter, it is impossible to know the number of attacks successfully deterred, a definition of success might consider whether national cybersecurity improves upon wider adoption of the strategic approach—but that definition itself is dependent on having metrics to evaluate the effectiveness of cybersecurity and cyberspace policy.[4]

For an example of the distinction between implementation and longer-term impact on cybersecurity, consider the Commission's Recommendation 1.3, calling for the establishment of a National Cyber Director. The FY21 NDAA legally requires the President to designate a National Cyber Director, and the first Director was confirmed on June 17, 2021.[5] This represents a major success in *implementation* of the recommendation, but its *successful impact* will be a function of how future presidents choose to empower and employ the Director. For this and all Commission recommendations, real success will depend on continuing momentum and impact long past the term of the Commission itself. With the distinction between implementation, impact, and success in mind, this assessment also looks to the future by outlining the steps needed to ensure that changes have lasting momentum.

---

4   The need for metrics to evaluate effectiveness in cybersecurity and cyber policy is also reflected in the Commission's recommendations. In particular, see Recommendation 4.3 – Establish a Bureau of Cyber Statistics, and Recommendation 6.1.6 – Require the Department of Defense to Define Reporting Metrics.

5   Tonya Riley, "Chris Inglis Confirmed as First US National Cyber Director after Senate Vote," *CyberScoop*, June 17, 2021, https://www.cyberscoop.com/chris-inglis-national-cyber-director-senate-vote/.

IDENTIFICATION OF THREATS, OPPORTUNITIES, AND PRIORITIES

The year 2020 threw more than its fair share of curveballs. In evaluating the future of the digital threat landscape, the Cyberspace Solarium Commission certainly did not anticipate all these twists and turns perfectly. Although the Commission's basic assumptions about threats, opportunities, and priorities bore out in the aggregate, hindsight does offer some lessons. Outlined below are the major dynamics that were not anticipated during the development of the Commission's original report.

Threats: The SolarWinds incident highlighted the importance of software supply chain security. Although a speculative evaluation suggests that some CSC recommendations might have helped mitigate the consequences of the event as it unfolded, many of those recommendations were not implemented until it occurred;[6] others still remain unimplemented. For example, the creation of a National Cybersecurity Certification and Labeling Authority (Recommendation 4.1) might have helped provide baseline levels of assurance to customers regarding the security of purchased ICT products. Similarly, a cloud security certification (Recommendation 4.5) might have also addressed some of the vulnerabilities that became apparent with respect to cloud service authentication. On the response side, certain recommendations, such as the codification of a Cyber State of Distress (Recommendation 3.3), would have granted the federal government additional response and recovery funds to assist state, local, tribal, and territorial (SLTT) governments and private-sector companies. In addition, in the wake of SolarWinds, renewed calls for federal breach notification (Recommendation 4.7.1) and incident reporting laws[7] (Recommendation 5.2.2) underscored the importance of recommendations that CSC made in its final report. Nevertheless, in retrospect it appears that CSC could have devoted more explicit attention to the issue of software supply chain security in its final report or its white paper on supply chain security, which was published in October 2020, just months before news broke about the SolarWinds incident.

Opportunities: The William M. (Mac) Thornberry National Defense Authorization Act for Fiscal Year 2021 (FY21 NDAA) reauthorized the CSC for an additional year, which has provided the Commission with more time than anticipated to push for the implementation of the March 2020 report's recommendations. Over this period, CSC has focused on updating legislative proposals for the coming NDAA cycle, encouraging appropriators to fund priorities authorized in the FY21 NDAA, and working on new white papers.

CSC's extended mandate also coincided with an election that created opportunities to engage a new administration and Congress and help set priorities for the coming years. CSC thus released a transition book for the Biden-Harris administration and was able to engage directly with the transition team and incoming appointees to help ensure that cybersecurity received the attention it deserves in the new administration's plans. The start of a new congressional session also created opportunities to implement CSC recommendations in new legislation and to engage with newly elected members of Congress as well as incumbent members assuming new leadership roles. The Senate-passed United States Innovation and Competition Act of 2021 (USICA) and the House-passed Cyber Diplomacy Act are important examples of how a new Congress, energized to tackle pressing issues, can champion new legislation.

---

6   For example, the executive order on improving the nation's cybersecurity implemented CSC Recommendation 4.4.3 on federal acquisition, and it touches on elements of Recommendations 4.1, 4.5, and others. Exec. Order No. 14028, "Improving the Nation's Cybersecurity," 86 Fed. Reg. 26633 (2021), https://www.federalregister.gov/documents/2021/05/17/2021-10460/improving-the-nations-cybersecurity. CSC Recommendation 3.3 was included in the U.S. Innovation and Competition Act (formerly Endless Frontier Act). The bill was passed by the Senate on June 8 and as of this writing awaits consideration in the House of Representatives. See United States Innovation and Competition Act of 2021 [hereafter USICA], S. 1260, § 4251-4252, 117th Cong. (2021), https://www.congress.gov/bill/117th-congress/senate-bill/1260/text/es.

7   Gopal Ratnam, "SolarWinds Incident May Bring Data Breach Notification Rules," Government Technology, March 3, 2021, https://www.govtech.com/security/solarwinds-incident-may-bring-data-breach-notification-rules.html.

Another unanticipated dynamic, although not one that constitutes an opportunity per se, was the increased focus on cybersecurity issues—and certain CSC recommendations—resulting from the SolarWinds hack, Microsoft Exchange Server hack, and, most recently, the Colonial Pipeline ransomware attack. As highlighted above, for example, the SolarWinds incident has renewed calls for national breach notification and incident reporting laws. Similarly, the pandemic, though devastating, has underscored the need for certain cybersecurity reforms that can aid both the federal government and SLTT governments in delivering digital services to American citizens. The American Rescue Plan Act included $650 million for the Cybersecurity and Infrastructure Security Agency (CISA), in recognition of the crucial role that cybersecurity plays at a time when the COVID-19 pandemic has forced Americans to shift economic, educational, and social activities online.

Priorities: CSC correctly focused attention on coordination and engagement with the private sector as a means of driving change. While that has always been a key priority, it is now even more crucial in the wake of the devastating SolarWinds, Microsoft, and Colonial Pipeline cyberattacks. The CSC's 2020 report noted that operationalizing this engagement with the private sector would enable the creation of a new "social contract" of shared responsibility in order to best secure the United States cyberspace.[8] Efforts to address this lack of coordination are evident through Pillar Five's specific focus on the private sector. Its recognition that "the majority of critical infrastructure, hardware, and software that powers the information age resides in the private sector" positioned CSC to see the private sector not as merely a regulatory subject but as an essential partner in the effort to deliver cybersecurity. For that reason, the private sector also plays a key role in Pillars Three and Four, and many of the recommendations in those pillars are designed to provide incentives for the private sector to improve its own cybersecurity and the security of products and services delivered to the public.

It is certainly true that events of the past year have not all unfolded as the Commission anticipated, but ongoing work has made possible further analysis and updates where initial assumptions or expectations proved incorrect. Throughout the past year, the Commission has continued to adjust to circumstances in a series of white papers. Both the Pandemic White Paper and the Supply Chain White Paper have provided opportunities to respond to new situations, including the COVID-19 pandemic, SolarWinds, Microsoft Exchange, and Colonial Pipeline attack. Meanwhile, an ongoing process to draft and propose legislation has enabled the Commission to continue to update the path of implementation for recommendations as conditions change.

EVALUATING THE IMPLEMENTATION OF THE LAYERED CYBER DETERRENCE STRATEGY

The Commission's layered cyber deterrence strategy itself provided a useful lens through which to consider the development of recommendations, and it has continued to provide helpful context in working through their implementation. Insofar as success can be defined as providing a coherent vision for the CSC's work, the strategic framework succeeded. A more general evaluation of whether it has been successful—both in being implemented and in driving improvements to national cybersecurity—will require a longer timeline and further development of metrics designed to assess cybersecurity.[9] An updated national cyber strategy will yield insight into implementation; but until an update is issued, the layered cyber deterrence approach can—at a minimum—give policymakers and government officials a means of thinking about the problem, especially when it comes to the broader implementation of "defend forward" across all instruments of national power.

---

8 U.S. Cyberspace Solarium Commission, *Report of the United States of America Cyberspace Solarium Commission* (March 2020), 96, https://www.solarium.gov/home.

9 The need for metrics to evaluate effectiveness in cybersecurity and cyber policy is also reflected in the Commission's recommendations. In particular, see Recommendation 4.3 – Establish a Bureau of Cyber Statistics, and Recommendation 6.1.6 – Require the Department of Defense to Define Reporting Metrics.

Cyber policy watchers have seen the unified exercise of different layers over the past year. For example, CISA has taken the lead on denying benefits by working with the private sector to build resilience, especially in the face of SolarWinds, while the White House imposes costs on adversary actors through sanctions and seeks to shape behavior through capacity-building projects.[10] While the administration may not use the term "layered cyber deterrence" to describe the suite of actions taken in response to cybersecurity crises, it has recognized that different tools of statecraft can work together, in concert, in response to specific threats and has generally taken a whole-of-nation approach to addressing the problem. In this respect, this strategy overall has been successful. To examine the state of implementation in further detail, this report considers examples at each layer of the strategy.

Shape Behavior

Strengthening U.S. cyber diplomacy at the State Department was chief among the recommendations proposed by the Commission to improve U.S. ability to shape behavior in cyberspace, and there has been clear progress toward this goal. The introduction of the Cyber Diplomacy Act, which was passed in the House of Representatives,[11] is an important step in the direction of developing this layer more thoroughly. The creation of a bureau at the State Department where U.S. strategy on cyber norms and international engagement on cyberspace issues can receive the attention and resources they deserve will position the United States well to shape the behavior of both allies and adversaries.

While improvements to the State Department's cyberspace policy structures would be major strides toward enhancing the U.S. ability to shape behavior, valuable work is already under way under the auspices of the Office of the Coordinator for Cyber Issues at the State Department, which has led U.S. cyber diplomacy since its creation in 2011.[12] The United States has historically been an influential and active participant at cyber norms forums like the U.N. Group of Governmental Experts and the U.N. Open-Ended Working Group.[13] Meanwhile, funding for international cybersecurity capacity building also received a modest increase for FY21 through the Consolidated Appropriations Act.[14] In short, progress is being made, but further efforts and sustained commitment in these areas are needed in order to effectively shape adversary behavior in cyberspace. Much more significant improvements to this layer of U.S. cyber deterrence are on the horizon.

Deny Benefits

By building more resilient systems nationwide and reducing the harm to the United States that can result from a cyberattack, effective deterrence denies adversaries the benefits of attacking. The majority of recommendations falling under three of the six pillars of the Solarium Commission's report focused on these types of changes (Pillars Three, Four, and Five).

---

10   "FACT SHEET: Imposing Costs for Harmful Foreign Activities by the Russian Government," White House Briefing Room, Press Release, April 15, 2021, https://www.whitehouse.gov/briefing-room/statements-releases/2021/04/15/fact-sheet-imposing-costs-for-harmful-foreign-activities-by-the-russian-government/.

11   Cyber Diplomacy Act of 2021, H.R. 1251, 117th Cong. (2021), https://www.congress.gov/bill/117th-congress/house-bill/1251.

12   "About Us – Office of the Coordinator for Cyber Issues," United States Department of State, https://www.state.gov/about-us-office-of-the-coordinator-for-cyber-issues/.

13   Christian Ruhl, Duncan Hollis, Wyatt Hoffman, and Tim Maurer, "Cyberspace and Geopolitics: Assessing Global Cybersecurity Norm Processes at a Crossroads," Carnegie Endowment for International Peace, February 26, 2020, https://carnegieendowment.org/2020/02/26/cyberspace-and-geopolitics-assessing-global-cybersecurity-norm-processes-at-crossroads-pub-81110.

14   U.S. Congress, Joint Explanatory Statement, Division F (to Accompany the Consolidated Appropriations Act, 2021), 116th Cong., 2nd sess. (2020), 51, https://docs.house.gov/billsthisweek/20201221/BILLS-116RCP68-JES-DIVISION-F.pdf.

One of the biggest successes with respect to denying benefits has been the inclusion of Continuity of the Economy planning in the FY21 NDAA. As outlined in the Commission's Recommendation 3.2, such a plan would dramatically decrease the impact of a cybersecurity attack—not to mention any other type of catastrophic event—through planning and preparation, thereby decreasing the incentive for adversaries to pursue such activity. Similarly, codifying sector-specific agencies (SSAs) as Sector Risk Management Agencies (SRMAs; Recommendation 3.1) has focused attention on how CISA can support federal departments and agencies in their efforts to build resilience by engaging the private sector. The establishment of the Joint Cyber Planning Office and study of an Integrated Cyber Center at CISA, which will focus, respectively, on coordinating cybersecurity readiness and planning between public and private sectors and on supporting the critical infrastructure security and resilience mission of the agency, are further noteworthy efforts in this area.

Denial of benefits also received significant attention in the CSC's white paper on supply chain security. Many of these recommendations have been implemented through the executive order on America's supply chains.[15] Other recommendations implemented in this area have yielded progress on developing an industrial base strategy, identifying key technologies, and designating a lead agency for coordinating supply chain risk management. In addition, recommendations from the original report such as requiring intelligence sharing within the Defense Industrial Base (DIB) (Recommendation 6.2.1) and threat hunting on DIB networks (Recommendation 6.2.2) contribute to the overall effort to deny benefits to adversary actors through improvements to the systems that underpin national cybersecurity.

While the Commission's work has been quite successful in driving overall progress on this layer of the strategy, challenges remain. Denying adversaries the benefits of attack requires extensive collaboration with the private sector and other stakeholders outside the federal government. Its multi-stakeholder nature makes this strategic layer quite complex to implement. In particular, three of the four recommendations proposed by the Commission that face significant known barriers to implementation fall under this layer of the strategy (3.3.2 – Clarify Liability for Federally Directed Mitigation, Response, and Recovery Efforts; 4.2 – Establish Liability for Final Goods Assemblers; and 4.7 – Pass a National Data Security and Privacy Protection Law). In the most difficult of cases, implementation may not be possible without significant shifts in opinion from major stakeholders. As major cybersecurity incidents continue to stack up, such a shift is not impossible. But in the meantime, the path forward will rest on continued engagement between sectors and stakeholders. While some elements of the "deny benefits" layer of the strategy have not yet been implemented, its prospects overall are very promising when the totality of the related recommendations are taken into account.

Impose Costs

Much of the attention devoted to this layer originates with recommendations from Pillar Six: Preserve and Employ the Military Instrument of Power. Many of these recommendations were put into law via the FY21 NDAA, making them successful in terms of their adoption. We need more time, however, to know whether that adoption will cause meaningful positive change. Promising steps toward implementation include NDAA language related to the Cyber Mission Force force structure assessment (Recommendation 6.1), assessing the establishment of a military cyber reserve (Recommendation 6.1.7), and studying potential vulnerabilities in weapons systems related to cybersecurity and emerging technologies like quantum computing (Recommendations 6.2 and 6.2.4). The Commission also saw major progress, albeit only partial implementation, with respect to efforts to create a Major Force Program (MFP) funding category for Cyber Command (Recommendation 6.1.1). With that said, not all of the U.S. ability to impose costs is military in nature. Other steps toward

---

15   Exec. Order No. 14017, "America's Supply Chains," 86 Fed. Reg. 11849 (2021), https://www.federalregister.gov/documents/2021/03/01/2021-04280/americas-supply-chains.

implementation of this layer of the strategic approach have come from the emphasis in Pillar Two on non-military tools for cost imposition. For example, the partial success in raising the number of FBI Cyber Assistant Legal Attachés (ALATs; part of Recommendation 2.1.4) increases the likelihood that bad actors are held accountable and face the consequences of violating the law.

Recent improvements to the structures and tools available to implement all three layers of a layered cyber deterrence strategy suggest that the United States is better positioned to employ the strategy now than it was a year ago. But because these changes are only just beginning to take effect, and others are yet to come, more information—and more time—is needed to successfully deter attacks of significant consequence in cyberspace. Moreover, more clearly defined metrics of cybersecurity and means of measuring effectiveness of cyberspace policy will be required to determine whether the strategy has been successful.

IMPLEMENTATION OF CSC RECOMMENDATIONS

The William M. (Mac) Thornberry National Defense Authorization Act for Fiscal Year 2021 (FY21 NDAA) adds to the mandate of the U.S. Cyberspace Solarium Commission by including the ongoing charge to review the implementation of the CSC's recommendations and provide an annual update.[16] While much work is yet required to fully implement CSC's recommendations, an interim review of progress shows that cybersecurity leaders throughout the government have taken significant steps. This report documents progress and identifies future actions required to advance the recommendations along the path toward protecting the United States from attacks of significant consequence in cyberspace. For the purposes of this assessment, indicators of progress toward implementation of Commission recommendations are varied but appear most frequently in authorizing legislation, appropriations, and executive policy.

Authorizing Legislation: The 2021 NDAA included a historic number of cybersecurity provisions, 27 of which represent the implementation of 25 different CSC recommendations. CSC will be supporting additional proposals during the course of its upcoming work. In July 2020, the Commission staff published a package of 54 legislative proposals,[17] many of which served as the starting point for legislation later included in the FY21 NDAA. Others are driving legislation expected to be proposed during the coming legislative cycle.

Appropriations: CSC highlighted 19 funding priorities during the FY21 appropriations cycle, many of which received funding in the Consolidated Appropriations Act of 2021.[18] Priorities not included or funded in the FY21 appropriations cycle, as well as those newly authorized in 2020, were included in recommendations to congressional appropriators for the FY22 cycle.

Executive Orders and Policy: In its "Transition Book for the Incoming Biden Administration," CSC outlined three priority areas of focus for the first hundred days, and an additional six priority areas for attention beyond one hundred days.

---

16   William M. (Mac) Thornberry National Defense Authorization Act for Fiscal Year 2021, Pub. L. No. 116-283 [hereafter FY21 NDAA], § 1714 (2021), available as enrolled bill at https://www.congress.gov/bill/116th-congress/house-bill/6395/text/enr.

17   Mark Montgomery, "Cyberspace Solarium Commission – Legislative Proposals," Cyberspace Solarium Commission, accessed March 22, 2021, https://www.solarium.gov/report/legislative-proposals.

18   For further information on the FY21 appropriations process, please see the joint explanatory statements provided by the House Rules Committee. House Committee on Rules, "Text of Bills for the Week of Dec. 21, 2020." December 21, 2020, https://docs.house.gov/floor/Default.aspx?date=2020-12-21.

Collectively, these areas represent 30 individual activities. Although at the time of this reporting the administration is still in its relatively early days, several of those actions are under way and are already being tracked by the Commission.

Other Actions: In some instances, indicators of progress fall outside the activities outlined above or government leaders are carrying the actions out in tandem with or anticipation of official legislation or policy. Furthermore, the Commission's recommendations were not made in a vacuum: they were the result of hundreds of conversations between Commissioners, staff, government representatives, subject matter experts, and many others. Consequently, many actions undertaken in cyberspace policy over the course of the past year both shaped and were shaped by Commission recommendations. Recognizing this dynamic, this assessment considers actions taken that align with CSC recommendations to be indicators of progress in implementing them, with the full appreciation that commendation for success in these—and all—cases is due to the hard work of cybersecurity and policy professionals in government and beyond. While these activities have not always been made public, the assessment below accounts for them to the extent possible.

In some cases, the recommendations face significant barriers to implementation that were anticipated even as they were drafted. While the Commission has focused heavily on shaping recommendations that had a clear path to implementation, it also recognized that limitations based on current circumstances should not inhibit its endorsement of ideas that could lead to dramatic improvement. Accordingly, the assessment below also contains four recommendations (marked in red) that are unlikely to overcome current barriers to implementation but that remain critical proposals, in the Commission's view.

Across the totality of actions included in these areas, progress toward implementation of each recommendation is given a single score as indicated by the following color-coding system:

IMPLEMENTATION STATUS
Implemented: Legislation has been passed, an executive order issued, or other definitive action taken.
Nearing Implementation: The recommendation is included in legislation or an executive order that has a clear path to approval, or it is partially implemented in law/policy.
On Track/Partial Implementation: The recommendation is being considered for a legislative vehicle, an executive order or other policy is being considered, or there are measurable/reported signs of progress.
Progress Limited/Delayed: The recommendation has not been rejected, but it is not in a legislative vehicle and there are no known policy actions under way.
Significant Barriers to Implementation: These recommendations are not expected to move in the immediate future but are ready to be taken up if future crises spur action.

THE FIRST 100 DAYS OF THE BIDEN-HARRIS ADMINISTRATION

In January of 2021, the Cyberspace Solarium Commission released its "Transition Book for the Incoming Biden Administration." This document outlined three areas on which the new administration should focus in its first hundred days:

1. Establish the Office of the National Cyber Director;
2. Develop and promulgate a National Cyber Strategy; and
3. Improve the coherence and impact of existing government cybersecurity efforts and further strengthen partnerships with the private sector.

That those first hundred days have recently drawn to a close provides an opportunity both to evaluate whether the priority areas identified by the Commission have been addressed and to note where executive action in general is trending toward the implementation of Commission recommendations. As we make this evaluation, the context of the past several months, which have been fraught with repeated cyber incidents, becomes particularly pertinent as well. The consequences of the SolarWinds compromise continue to unfold, even as major vulnerabilities are exploited in Microsoft Exchange Servers and as ransomware usage explodes, shutting down major critical infrastructure. The administration should be commended for responding to these exigent circumstances—a monumental task—and progress in the response is evident in the May 12, 2021, executive order on improving the nation's cybersecurity.[19] While the demands of wrestling with these specific incidents have undoubtedly drawn time and attention away from other aspects of policymaking, they have also demonstrated the need for the coordination, coherence, and strategic guidance that improved policies could bring.

Efforts to address these three CSC 100-day priorities are under way to varying degrees, but only the first—establishing the Office of the National Cyber Director—is clearly on track to implementation, as is discussed at length below. Meanwhile, a new national cyber strategy has not been released but is reportedly in process.[20] The Interim National Security Strategic Guidance states that the administration "will elevate cybersecurity as an imperative across the government," and will encourage collaboration between the public and private sectors.[21] While the final result of the strategy development is not yet known, it is clear that its intent aligns with the Commission's priorities for executive action.

---

19 Exec. Order No. 14028.

20 Subcommittee on Cyber, Innovative Technologies, and Information Systems Hearing: *"Operations in Cyberspace and Building Cyber Capabilities Across the Department of Defense,"* 117th Cong. (2021) (testimony of Mieke Eoyang and Paul M. Nakasone) https://armedservices.house.gov/hearings?ID=A29B4BAE-E25A-4ABF-B0AF-8C1F089EF2E0.

21 Joseph R. Biden, Jr., "Interim National Security Strategic Guidance" (March 2021), 18, https://www.whitehouse.gov/wp-content/uploads/2021/03/NSC-1v2.pdf.

Beyond the priorities established in the Commission's transition book, early activity from the executive branch suggests progress on other CSC recommendations. One particular example is the February 2021 executive order on America's supply chains,[22] which made major steps toward implementing the Commission's Recommendations 4.6 and 4.6.1, as well as the recommendations from the CSC white paper "Building a Trusted ICT Supply Chain." The executive order initiated a series of reports that align with the first steps of the Commission's recommendations for developing an information communication technology supply chain strategy. Similarly, the establishment of a cybersecurity working group involving the United States, Japan, India, and Australia, formed in March 2021,[23] is a major step towards implementing the activities described in Commission Recommendation 2.1.1, which calls for international engagement to strengthen norms of responsible state behavior.

The President's Budget Request provides further insight into the Biden administration's early priorities. Overall, the request strengthens cybersecurity and particularly focuses on protecting federal civilian networks by requesting a nearly 15 percent increase in funding for cybersecurity in federal civilian agencies, on top of a nearly 11 percent increase achieved in 2020 by the Trump administration.[24] This willingness to invest signals that the issue is being made a real priority; however, funding for the federal government's work as an enabler of better cybersecurity nationwide—beyond federal networks—is less evident in the request. For example, the Cybersecurity and Infrastructure Security Agency saw an increase of just under $110 million, about 5 percent.[25] As a point of comparison, in a letter to the congressional appropriations committees, Commissioners recommended an increase of $400 million. Similarly, the budget for cybersecurity and privacy at the National Institute of Standards and Technology (NIST), which develops and maintains several resources that have become keystones of national and even global cybersecurity best practice, recommends an increase of only 6 percent, bringing the total to $81.9 million. Notably, the President recommends an increase in NIST's overall budget of almost 45 percent.[26] In the aggregate, it is apparent that the administration is taking investment in the cybersecurity of federal networks seriously, but more is needed to reflect the government's role as an enabler of national cybersecurity.

As is clear from the assessment below, these steps forward are being taken in only a few of many different areas that call for executive action. The U.S. government has a lot of work ahead. However, the early progress under the leadership of the Deputy National Security Advisor for Cyber and Emerging Technology is very encouraging; and as other key cybersecurity leaders—particularly the Director of the Cybersecurity and Infrastructure Security Agency, the head of State Department's cyberspace policy, and especially the National Cyber Director—officially take office, the Commission expects to see more indicators of progress toward the implementation of recommendations that require executive action.

22   Exec. Order No. 14017.

23   "Press Briefing by Press Secretary Jen Psaki and National Security Advisor Jake Sullivan," The White House, March 12, 2021, https://www.whitehouse.gov/briefing-room/press-briefings/2021/03/12/press-briefing-by-press-secretary-jen-psaki-march-12-2021/.

24   United States Office of Management and Budget, *Analytical Perspectives: Budget of the U.S. Government, Fiscal Year 2022*, (Washington, DC, U.S. Government Publishing Office, 2021), 168, https://www.whitehouse.gov/wp-content/uploads/2021/05/spec_fy22.pdf.

25   United States Department of Homeland Security, *Cybersecurity and Infrastructure Security Agency: Budget Overview, Fiscal Year 2022* (Washington, DC, 2021), 8, https://www.dhs.gov/sites/default/files/publications/cybersecurity_and_infrastructure_security_agency_0.pdf.

26   United States Department of Commerce, *National Institute of Standards and Technology, National Technical Information Service: Fiscal Year 2022 Budget Submission to Congress* (Washington, DC, 2021), 8, https://www.commerce.gov/sites/default/files/2021-06/fy2022_nist_congressional_budget_justification.pdf.

RECOMMENDATIONS FROM THE CYBERSPACE SOLARIUM COMMISSION REPORT

The U.S. Cyberspace Solarium Commission Report, issued in March of 2020, presents 82 recommendations separated into six thematic pillars. Proceeding by pillar, this section outlines progress on each recommendation. Recommendations listed in the original report as "Key Recommendations" are indicated in bold in the charts displayed below.

PILLAR ONE: REFORM THE U.S. GOVERNMENT'S STRUCTURE AND ORGANIZATION FOR CYBERSPACE

Assessment of Overall Pillar Progress

Pillar One of the CSC report highlights one of the Commission's flagship recommendations: the establishment of a National Cyber Director (Recommendation 1.3). Section 1752 in the FY21 National Defense Authorization Act established the position in law, a step that was further advanced when the Biden administration announced a nomination for the position on April 12, 2021 and a Director was confirmed on June 17, 2021. Recommendation 1.4, which focuses on strengthening CISA, is similarly crucial. The recommendation represents several different related actions, four of which were enacted into law in the FY21 NDAA. Overall, significant steps have been taken toward implementation of the Commission's recommendations in this pillar, but as emphasized above, there is a distinction between implementation and success. Even for these major achievements, the manner in which the law is carried out will significantly impact the overall success of these recommendations in making meaningful, lasting improvements in national cybersecurity. Moreover, other prominent recommendations from this pillar remain to be implemented. Funding for cyber workforce development programs in the National Science Foundation (NSF), NIST, and CISA, in particular, will be a key priority for the coming months.

Rec. Number	Recommendation Title	Status	Assessment
—	REFORM THE U.S. GOVERNMENT'S STRUCTURE AND ORGANIZATION FOR CYBERSPACE		
1.1	Issue an Updated National Cyber Strategy	In Process	🟩
1.1.1	Develop a Multitiered Signaling Strategy	Executive Action Needed	🟨
1.1.2	Promulgate a New Declaratory Policy	Executive Action Needed	🟧
1.2	**Create House Permanent Select and Senate Select Committees on Cybersecurity**	Faces Significant Barriers to Implementation	🟥
1.2.1	Reestablish the Office of Technology Assessment	Appropriations Needed	🟨
1.3	Establish National Cyber Director (NCD)	Legislation Passed in FY21 NDAA, NCD Confirmed, Related Executive Order Issued, Requires Appropriations	🟩

1.4	Strengthen the Cybersecurity and Infrastructure Security Agency	Legislation Passed in FY21 NDAA, Related Executive Order Issued	🟩
1.4.1	Codify and Strengthen the Cyber Threat Intelligence Integration Center	Legislation Proposed; Appropriations Needed	🟧
1.4.2	Strengthen the FBI's Cyber Mission and the National Cyber Investigative Joint Task Force	Appropriations Needed	🟨
1.5	Diversify and Strengthen the Federal Cyberspace Workforce	Partially Implementation via Legislation Passed in FY21 NDAA; Further Legislation and Appropriations Needed	🟨
1.5.1	Improve Cyber-Oriented Education	Appropriations Needed	🟩

Recommendation Progress

Recommendation 1.1 – Issue an Updated National Cyber Strategy: This recommendation will require executive action. While the Biden-Harris administration has indicated that cybersecurity will be an early priority,[27] a new National Cyber Strategy has yet to be released. At a May 14 hearing before the House Armed Services' Subcommittee on Cyber, Innovative Technologies, and Information Systems, Deputy Assistant Secretary of Defense for Cyber Policy Mieke Eoyang indicated that the Biden administration is currently conducting the review that will culminate in the issuance of a new National Cyber Strategy.[28] Separately, CSC staff have offered the administration text for an executive order, providing further specificity in fulfilling the recommendation.

Recommendation 1.1.1 – Develop a Multitiered Signaling Strategy: This recommendation will require executive action, and CSC staff have drafted text for an executive order that outlines a detailed plan for developing a multitiered signaling strategy aimed at altering adversaries' decision calculus and addressing the risks of escalation in cyber conflicts. Recent action from the Biden administration, including the June 2021 meeting with Russian President Vladimir Putin,[29] demonstrates a willingness to engage in signaling through individual engagements, but does not—in and of itself—demonstrate a multitiered signaling strategy.

Recommendation 1.1.2 – Promulgate a New Declaratory Policy: This recommendation will require executive action. CSC staff have drafted text for an executive order that reforms the United States' declaratory policy regarding cyberspace and is focused on a use-of-force threshold in order to reinforce deterrence of strategic cyberattacks.

Recommendation 1.2 – Create House Permanent Select and Senate Select Committees on Cybersecurity: The Commission expected and has encountered significant pressure against this recommendation, which is one of the four that face known significant barriers to implementation. However, the recommendation has been drafted into legislative language and stands ready should a future emergency create the political impetus needed to overcome existing barriers.

---

27   Maggie Miller, "Biden: US Taking 'Urgent' Steps to Improve Cybersecurity," *The Hill*, (February 4, 2021), https://thehill.com/policy/cybersecurity/537436-biden-says-administration-launching-urgent-initiative-to-improve-nations.

28   Eoyang, testimony at hearing, "Operations in Cyberspace and Building Cyber Capabilities Across the Department of Defense," at 20:18.

29   Vladimir Soldatkin and Humeyra Pamuk, "Biden Tells Putin Certain Cyberattacks Should Be 'Off-limits,'" *Reuters*, June 16, 2021, https://www.reuters.com/technology/biden-tells-putin-certain-cyber-attacks-should-be-off-limits-2021-06-16/.

Recommendation 1.2.1 – Reestablish the Office of Technology Assessment: The Office of Technology Assessment is already authorized, and requires only the appropriation of funds to implement the recommendation. CSC's Commissioners who are members of Congress submitted a letter to the appropriations committees recommending $6 million for this purpose in FY21; however, the joint explanatory statement accompanying the FY21 appropriations bill recommended additional funding to support the development of technological expertise in the Government Accountability Office (GAO) and the Congressional Research Service.[30] Because both these organizations function by responding to specific reporting requests, they cannot maintain the in-the-moment expertise needed by legislators and their staffs. Accordingly, for FY22 the CSC's congressional Commissioners repeated their recommendation for $6 million to fund the Office of Technology Assessment.

Recommendation 1.3 – Establish National Cyber Director: The position of National Cyber Director was established in Section 1752 of the FY21 NDAA, and the Biden administration nominated Cyberspace Solarium Commissioner Chris Inglis as the first to serve in the post.[31] The Homeland Security and Governmental Affairs Committee in the Senate held a confirmation hearing on June 10, 2021, and Inglis was confirmed as National Cyber Director on June 17, 2021.[32] Executive branch leaders can continue to ensure adherence—both in letter and in spirit—to the law establishing this position by empowering the National Cyber Director to coordinate, support, and deconflict whole-of-nation cybersecurity and defensive cyber efforts. Taking steps in this direction, Executive Order 14028 ("Improving the Nation's Cybersecurity") clarifies that upon the appointment of the NCD and the establishment of the related office, portions of the order may be modified to ensure that the NCD can execute his duties. The CSC's congressional Commissioners submitted a letter to the appropriations committees during the FY22 appropriations cycle recommending that $50 million in funding be provided for this purpose, with half of that available through FY23. The President's Budget Request includes $15 million to establish the Office of the National Cyber Director.[33]

Recommendation 1.4 – Strengthen the Cybersecurity and Infrastructure Security Agency: This recommendation, composed of several elements, was largely put into law in Sections 1705, 1718, 1745, and 9001 of the FY21 NDAA. The Biden administration's recent executive order on improving the nation's cybersecurity further strengthens CISA by implementing such efforts as cyber vulnerability reduction, incident response planning for the federal government, and the creation of an endpoint detection and response (EDR) initiative to bolster federal government capability to detect incidents.[34] The remaining element of the Commission's recommendation not yet implemented is a five-year term for the Director of the Cybersecurity and Infrastructure Security Agency. The Commission will be pursuing this legislative objective in the coming months. Moreover, during the FY21 appropriations cycle the CSC's congressional Commissioners submitted a letter to the appropriations committees recommending an increase in funding for CISA to bolster mission support activities (an increase

30 U.S. Congress, Joint Explanatory Statement, Division I (to Accompany the Consolidated Appropriations Act, 2021), 116th Cong., 2nd sess. (2020), 2, https://docs.house.gov/billsthisweek/20201221/BILLS-116RCP68-JES-DIVISION-I.pdf.

31 "Statement by National Security Advisor Jake Sullivan on National Cyber Director and CISA Director Nominations," White House Briefing Room, April 12, 2021, https://www.whitehouse.gov/briefing-room/statements-releases/2021/04/12/statement-by-national-security-advisor-jake-sullivan-on-national-cyber-director-and-cisa-director-nominations/.

32 H*omeland Security and Governmental Affairs Committee Hearing, "Nominations of Robin Carnahan to be Administrator, General Services Administration; Jen Easterly to be Director, Cybersecurity and Infrastructure Security Agency, DHS; and Chris Inglis to be National Cyber Director,"* 117th Cong. (2021), https://www.hsgac.senate.gov/hearings/nominations-of-robin-carnahan-to-be-administrator-general-services-administration-jen-easterly-to-be-director-cybersecurity-and-infrastructure-security-agency-dhs-and-chris-inglis-to-be-national-cyber-director; Riley, "Chris Inglis Confirmed as First US National Cyber Director."

33 Office of Management and Budget, *Budget of the U.S. Government: Fiscal Year 2022* (Washington, DC: U.S. Government Publishing Office, 2021), 32, https://www.whitehouse.gov/wp-content/uploads/2021/05/budget_fy22.pdf.

34 Exec. Order No. 14028.

of approximately $56.5 million over FY20 enacted levels) and support additional hunt and incident response teams (an increase of $40 million). The large majority of the mission support activities were funded in the FY21 appropriations bill, but only $3 million was provided to increase CISA's threat-hunting capabilities. The CSC's congressional Commissioners recommended additional funding for CISA during the FY22 appropriations cycle. The request included an increase of $400 million to the 050 National Defense Budget Function, from which CISA draws almost all of its funding, in order to augment the overall share of money that can be allocated to CISA during the appropriations process.

Recommendation 1.4.1 – Codify and Strengthen the Cyber Threat Intelligence Integration Center (CTIIC): CSC staff have proposed legislation in support of this recommendation. Since the CTIIC was established in 2015, it has consistently been underresourced, lacking the funds, manpower, and analytical assets it needs to carry out its mission. Legislative action and subsequent appropriations are needed to implement this recommendation.

Recommendation 1.4.2 – Strengthen the FBI's Cyber Mission and the National Cyber Investigative Joint Task Force: The implementation of this recommendation requires additional funding. During the FY21 appropriations cycle, the CSC's congressional Commissioners submitted a letter to the appropriations committees recommending an increase in funding to the Federal Bureau of Investigation Cyber Division of $28.5 million above the FY20 enacted level, and $17 million above the presidential FY21 request. The FY21 appropriations bill did not follow this recommendation. The CSC's congressional Commissioners have again recommended funding support for these critical functions in the FY22 appropriations cycle, and the President's Budget Request includes $40 million to "increase the FBI's capacity for unilateral, joint, and enabled [cyber] operations with other Federal, State, local and international partners."[35]

Recommendation 1.5 – Diversify and Strengthen the Federal Cyberspace Workforce: Legislation passed in the FY21 NDAA partially met this recommendation but requires an increase in appropriations to enable the newly authorized work (Sections 9401–9407), and the Federal Cybersecurity Workforce Expansion Act, introduced in June 2021, would implement elements of the recommendation related to federal apprenticeship and veteran upskilling programs if passed.[36] Further authorization is needed to implement other elements of the recommendation. The CSC's congressional Commissioners submitted a letter to the appropriations committees recommending an increase in funding during the FY21 appropriations cycle of $20 million above the FY20 enacted level in order to grow the CyberCorps: Scholarship for Service program. The FY21 appropriations bill provided an additional $5 million over FY20 enacted levels, stipulating that $7.5 million must be used to support a specific subset of programs. For FY22, the President's Budget Request has recommended a $10 million increase to the program's budget.[37] However, to ensure future growth of this critical federal cyber workforce program commensurate with the need for cyber professionals, the CSC's congressional Commissioners have recommended an additional increase of $20 million for the FY22 appropriations cycle.

Recommendation 1.5.1 – Improve Cyber-Oriented Education: To support the provision of curricula, educator training, and other resources to improve cybersecurity education nationwide, CSC supported the codification of the Cybersecurity Education and Training Assistance Program (CETAP), which was implemented through Section 1719 of the FY21 NDAA.

---

35   Department of Justice, "Federal Bureau of Investigation (FBI): FY 2022 Budget Request at a Glance," Department of Justice, 122, https://www.justice.gov/jmd/page/file/1399031/download.

36   "Senators Hassan, Cornyn Introduce Bipartisan Bill to Strengthen Federal Cyber Workforce," Office of Senator Maggie Hassan, June 25, 2021, https://www.hassan.senate.gov/news/press-releases/senators-hassan-cornyn-introduce-bipartisan-bill-to-strengthen-federal-cyber-workforce.

37   National Science Foundation, *National Science Foundation: FY 2022 Budget Request to Congress* (May 2021), 48, https://www.nsf.gov/about/budget/fy2022/pdf/fy2022budget.pdf.

The President's Budget Request for FY22 suggested eliminating the budget for this program.[38] The CSC's congressional Commissioners also submitted a letter to the appropriations committees recommending additional funding for this program in the FY22 appropriations cycle.

PILLAR TWO: STRENGTHEN NORMS AND NON-MILITARY TOOLS

Assessment of Overall Pillar Progress

Progress toward implementation of Pillar Two recommendations largely took the form of building momentum via public engagement for legislation in the upcoming months, though funding a portion of the recommended Cyber ALATs in the FBI is a significant accomplishment in its own right. In February of 2021, the Cyber Diplomacy Act was reintroduced in the House of Representatives, and its co-sponsors included two CSC Commissioners. This legislation would implement the key Recommendation 2.1 of this pillar by establishing the Bureau of International Cyberspace Policy led by an ambassador, reporting to the Undersecretary of State for Policy or a higher State Department official. As of the time of publication, the bill has passed the House and has been received in the Senate. Passage of this legislation would represent major progress for this pillar, and will remain a major priority for the Commission in 2021. An additional priority for 2021 is the consolidation of capacity-building funds as outlined in Recommendation 2.1.3. Capacity building incentivizes and enables countries to abide by norms of responsible state behavior and thereby improves cybersecurity globally, but its effective implementation requires the flexibility and comprehensive approach of a consolidated fund.

STRENGTHEN NORMS AND NON-MILITARY TOOLS			
Rec. Number	Recommendation Title	Status	Assessment
2.1	Create a Cyber Bureau and Assistant Secretary at the U.S. Department of State	Legislation Has Passed in the House	🟩
2.1.1	Strengthen Norms of Responsible State Behavior in Cyberspace	Executive Actions Taken; Executive Order Proposed	🟨
2.1.2	Engage Actively and Effectively in Forums Setting International Information and Communications Technology Standards	Legislation Has Passed in the Senate; Appropriations Needed	🟨
2.1.3	Improve Cyber Capacity Building and Consolidate the Funding of Cyber Foreign Assistance	Legislation Proposed; Appropriations Needed	🟨
2.1.4	Improve International Tools for Law Enforcement Activities in Cyberspace	Legislation Proposed; Appropriations Needed	🟩
2.1.5	Leverage Sanctions and Trade Enforcement Actions	Legislation Proposed	🟨
2.1.6	Improve Attribution Analysis and the Attribution-Decision Rubric	Executive Order Proposed	🟧
2.1.7	Reinvigorate Efforts to Develop Cyber Confidence-Building Measures	Executive Order Proposed	🟧

---

38   U.S. Department of Homeland Security, *Cybersecurity and Infrastructure Security Agency: Budget Overview, Fiscal Year 2022*, 154.

Recommendation Progress

Recommendation 2.1 — Create a Cyber Bureau and Assistant Secretary at the U.S. Department of State: CSC staff have proposed legislation in support of this recommendation, and the Cyber Diplomacy Act of 2021, which closely aligns with the CSC's proposal, was introduced on February 23, 2021, and passed in the House of Representatives on April 20, 2021.[39] The Cyber Diplomacy Act recommends the creation of the Bureau of International Cyberspace Policy and, if passed, will meet the intent of the Commission's recommendation; the bureau will require additional appropriations to be fully funded and resourced.

Recommendation 2.1.1 – Strengthen Norms of Responsible State Behavior in Cyberspace: This recommendation will require executive action, and CSC staff have provided text to the administration for a draft executive order that outlines actions federal departments and agencies can take to accomplish this recommendation through diplomatic engagement, expanded capacity building, and reinvigorated confidence-building measures. Recent executive actions demonstrate that steps implementing this recommendation are at least partially underway. The establishment of a working group announced in March involving the United States, Japan, India, and Australia is a major step toward international engagement to strengthen norms of responsible state behavior,[40] and certainly shows that these issues have been elevated to the level of head-of-state conversations. However, many more steps such as these will need to be taken if this recommendation is to be fully implemented.

Recommendation 2.1.2 – Engage Actively and Effectively in Forums Setting International Information and Communications Technology Standards: Executive action and appropriations are required for this recommendation. To address both the requirements of this recommendation and the related requirements in Recommendation 4.1.2 below, the CSC's congressional Commissioners submitted a letter to the appropriations committees recommending an increase in funding of $30 million for FY21 to support NIST's cybersecurity and privacy programs. The Consolidated Appropriations Act for FY21 did not include this increase, though the requirements for work on standards have grown rapidly. Accordingly, the CSC's congressional Commissioners have recommended a significant increase to support NIST's cybersecurity and privacy programs for FY22. The President's FY22 Budget Request includes a modest increase (approximately $2.35 million) for the Standards Coordination and Special Programs portfolio, which includes NIST's work on international standards development,[41] as well as increases totaling $3.5 million that would benefit specific standards initiatives in the areas of advanced communications and would help strengthen diversity and equity in the standards workforce.[42] Separately, the Senate-passed USICA includes several provisions that make progress on this issue. Section 2306 would require the Secretary of Commerce to work with the Secretary of Energy to build capacity and training programs for U.S. engagement in standards setting, partner with the private sector on developing standards for digital economy technologies, and prioritize efforts focused on developing standards for emerging technologies. Section 3210 requires the President to establish an interagency working group, led by the Secretary of State, whose goal is to increase U.S. engagement in international standards bodies focused on 5G. The working group would also be assigned responsibility for providing a strategy that addresses U.S. engagement at 5G standards

39   "Meeks, McCaul, Gallagher, Langevin, Kinzinger, Keating Reintroduce the Cyber Diplomacy Act," U.S. House of Representatives Committee on Foreign Affairs – Press Releases, February 23, 2021, https://foreignaffairs.house.gov/2021/2/meeks-mccaul-gallagher-langevin-kinzinger-keating-reintroduce-the-cyber-diplomacy-act; Vavra, "House Green Lights New State Department Cyber Bureau."

40   "Press Briefing by Psaki and Sullivan."

41   Department of Commerce, *National Institute of Standards and Technology, National Technical Information Service: Fiscal Year 2022 Budget Submission to Congress* (June 2021), 80, https://www.commerce.gov/sites/default/files/2021-06/fy2022_nist_congressional_budget_justification.pdf.

42   Department of Commerce, *NIST Fiscal Year 2022 Budget Submission to Congress*, 81–84, 90–92.

bodies, diplomatic engagement with partners and allies, China's presence and engagement at standards bodies, and engagement with private-sector stakeholders to develop 5G standards. Other provisions direct the Assistant Secretary of Commerce for Communications and Information to prepare a briefing on barriers to robust U.S. government participation in standards activities at the International Telecommunication Union and on opportunities for further participation, authorize a grant program to encourage private-sector participation at standards bodies, and direct the Secretary of State to establish a regular dialogue with partners and allies on international regulatory issues, including standards setting.[43]

Recommendation 2.1.3 – Improve Cyber Capacity Building and Consolidate the Funding of Cyber Foreign Assistance: Legislation and appropriations are needed to achieve this outcome. CSC staff have provided a legislative proposal that would consolidate foreign assistance in support of efforts to build cyber capacity. In addition, the CSC's congressional Commissioners submitted a letter to the appropriations committees for FY21 recommending $10 million in increased funding for cyber capacity building. The FY21 NDAA authorized a military cyber capacity building program under Department of Defense authorities specific to Vietnam, Thailand, and Indonesia (Section 1256); the Consolidated Appropriations Act for FY21 included $7 million for capacity building through the Office of the Coordinator for Cyber Issues, which was repeated in the FY22 President's Budget Request.[44] In order to maintain these existing programs while also addressing new and emerging priorities, the CSC's congressional Commissioners recommended an increase in funds for multiple foreign assistance accounts to be appropriated for FY22 for cybersecurity capacity building at the State Department. USICA may also enable progress in this area, as a provision of the proposed legislation would authorize $100 million in funding annually for FY22–26 in support of the Digital Connectivity and Cybersecurity Partnership, which aims in part to build cybersecurity capacity in foreign countries.[45]

Recommendation 2.1.4 – Improve International Tools for Law Enforcement Activities in Cyberspace: The CSC has put forward two elements in support of this recommendation. The first is a legislative proposal from the CSC staff that aims to grant subpoena authority to the Office of International Affairs at the Department of Justice in order to streamline the execution of Mutual Legal Assistance Treaties and Mutual Legal Assistance Agreements, and congressional action is needed to pass the proposed legislation. The second aims to increase the number of Cyber Assistant Legal Attachés serving the FBI from 10 to 22. The CSC's congressional Commissioners therefore submitted a letter to the appropriations committees recommending that the funding level for FY21 be set at $17.6 million. Six additional attachés were funded in FY21, but further appropriations are needed to support the remaining positions. The CSC's congressional Commissioners recommended an increase in appropriations for FY22 in support of these positions.

Recommendation 2.1.5 – Leverage Sanctions and Trade Enforcement Actions: In support of this recommendation, CSC staff proposed legislation that codifies Executive Order 13848, which allows for the imposition of sanctions in the event of foreign election interference.[46] The legislative proposal mandates an assessment and report on foreign election interference and a subsequent assessment of the extent to which any such identified interference materially affected the security or integrity of

43   USICA, §§ 2517, 2520, 3208.

44   U.S. Department of State, *Congressional Budget Justification: Department of State, Foreign Operations, and Related Programs: Fiscal Year 2022* (May 2021), 144, https://www.state.gov/wp-content/uploads/2021/05/FY-2022-State_USAID-Congressional-Budget-Justification.pdf.

45   USICA, § 3122.

46   Exec. Order No. 13848, "Imposing Certain Sanctions in the Event of Foreign Interference in a United States Election," 86 Fed. Reg. 46843 (2018), https://www.federalregister.gov/documents/2018/09/14/2018-20203/imposing-certain-sanctions-in-the-event-of-foreign-interference-in-a-united-states-election.

election infrastructure or the infrastructure of a political organization, campaign, or candidate.[47] Legislative action is needed to further implement the recommendation. Separately, the administration has recently imposed sanctions against Russian actors in response to the Foreign Intelligence Service's involvement in the compromise of SolarWinds and other information technology infrastructures.[48]

Recommendation 2.1.6 – Improve Attribution Analysis and the Attribution-Decision Rubric: This recommendation requires executive action, and CSC staff have provided text to the administration for a draft executive order laying out what federal departments and agencies should do. The draft executive order outlines processes for convening incident-triggered Cybersecurity Incident Attribution Analysis Working Groups, aimed at coordinating the task of attribution in the wake of a cyber incident. The draft executive order also mandates the creation of a Cyber Incident Attribution and Analysis Decision Rubric, which correlates appropriate U.S. government response actions to cyberattacks with levels of confidence in assigning attribution.

Recommendation 2.1.7 – Reinvigorate Efforts to Develop Cyber Confidence-Building Measures: This recommendation will require executive action, and CSC staff have provided text to the administration for a draft executive order that outlines actions to be taken by the State Department, including engaging with diplomats at international cyber norms forums, undertaking bilateral and multilateral accords, and encouraging like-minded countries to similarly engage in such forums and processes.

PILLAR THREE: PROMOTE NATIONAL RESILIENCE

Assessment of Overall Pillar Progress

The passage of the National Defense Authorization Act for FY2021 made dramatic progress in the implementation of this pillar, most particularly by beginning work on the development of a Continuity of the Economy plan (Recommendation 3.2 and NDAA Section 9603) and the establishment of Sector Risk Management Agencies (Recommendation 3.1 and NDAA Section 9002). However, significant work remains. First, these critical steps forward must be funded through appropriations, now that they have been authorized. Second, the Commission must prioritize advancing the next tranche of priorities. Establishing the National Cybersecurity Assistance Fund (Recommendation 3.1.2) will remain a key priority for authorizing legislation, while funding existing programs that advance civics education as a means of countering disinformation (part of Recommendation 3.5) will be a key priority in the Commission's recommendations to congressional appropriators.

PROMOTE NATIONAL RESILIENCE			
Rec. Number	Recommendation Title	Status	Assessment
3.1	Codify Sector-specific Agencies as SRMAs and Strengthen Their Ability to Manage Critical Infrastructure Risk	Legislation Passed in FY21 NDAA; Appropriations Needed	
3.1.1	Establish a National Risk Management Cycle Culminating in a Critical Infrastructure Resilience Strategy	Executive Order Proposed; Legislation Has Passed in the Senate	

---

47 CSC Staff, *Legislative Proposals* (2020), 53, https://drive.google.com/file/d/1S5N7KvjFfxow19kCnPl0nx7Mah8pK0uG/view.

48 White House, "FACT SHEET: Imposing Costs for Harmful Foreign Activities by the Russian Government."

3.1.2	Establish a National Cybersecurity Assistance Fund	Legislation Proposed	
3.2	Develop and Maintain Continuity of the Economy Planning	Legislation Passed in FY21 NDAA; Appropriations Needed	
3.3	Codify a "Cyber State of Distress" Tied to a "Cyber Response and Recovery Fund"	Legislation Has Passed in the Senate	
3.3.1	Designate Responsibilities for Cybersecurity Services under the Defense Production Act	Faces Significant Barriers to Implementation	
3.3.2	Clarify Liability for Federally Directed Mitigation, Response, and Recovery Efforts	Legislation Proposed	
3.3.3	Improve and Expand Planning Capacity and Readiness for Cyber Incident Response and Recovery Efforts	Executive Order Proposed, Related Executive Order Issued	
3.3.4	Expand Coordinated Cyber Exercises, Gaming, and Simulation	Appropriations Met in FY21 Omnibus	
3.3.5	Establish a Biennial National Cyber Tabletop Exercise	Legislation Passed in FY21 NDAA; Appropriations Needed	
3.3.6	Clarify the Cyber Capabilities and Strengthen the Interoperability of the National Guard	Legislation Passed in FY21 NDAA; Appropriations Needed	
3.4	Improve the Structure and Enhance Funding of the Election Assistance Commission	Legislation Passed in the House; Appropriations Needed	
3.4.1	Modernize Campaign Regulations to Promote Cybersecurity	Legislation Proposed	
3.5	Build Societal Resilience to Foreign Malign Cyber-Enabled Information Operations	Legislation Proposed; Appropriations Needed	
3.5.1	Reform Online Political Advertising to Defend against Foreign Influence in Elections	Legislation Proposed	

Recommendation Progress

Recommendation 3.1 – Codify Sector-specific Agencies into Law as "Sector Risk Management Agencies" and Strengthen Their Ability to Manage Critical Infrastructure Risk: The FY21 NDAA codified sector-specific agencies into law as Sector Risk Management Agencies (Section 9002). The CSC's congressional Commissioners submitted a letter to the appropriations committees recommending two funding increases for FY21 in support of this recommendation. The first increase was to support CISA's management efforts across all sector-specific agencies—now Sector Risk Management Agencies, and the second was to support the Office of Cybersecurity and Critical Infrastructure Protection (OCCIP) at the Department of the Treasury, which serves as the Sector Risk Management Agency for financial services. The first was partially realized through the Consolidated Appropriations Act for FY21, but the second was not. The CSC's congressional Commissioners recommended further appropriations in FY22 to carry out this original recommendation.

Recommendation 3.1.1 – Establish a National Risk Management Cycle Culminating in a Critical Infrastructure Resilience Strategy: Implementation of this recommendation will require legislative action to direct the executive branch to conduct an initial risk identification and assessment of critical infrastructure based on currently defined national critical functions and to establish processes and procedures to establish a recurring National Risk Management Cycle. Legislation that would meet the intent of this recommendation is already underway. In April 2021, Senators Maggie Hassan and Ben Sasse introduced the National Risk Management Act of 2021, which would implement this recommendation.[49] The bill has been folded into USICA;[50] it would require the Secretary of Homeland Security, acting through the Director of CISA, to establish a recurring process for identifying, assessing, and prioritizing both risks to critical infrastructure (including both cyber and physical threats) and the resources needed to address such risks. Once an initial report identifying such risks has been produced, the President must deliver a national critical infrastructure resilience strategy, and the Secretary of Homeland Security must annually brief Congress on activities taken pursuant to the strategy.

Recommendation 3.1.2 – Establish a National Cybersecurity Assistance Fund: CSC staff have proposed legislation in support of this recommendation to establish a National Cybersecurity Assistance Fund for programs and projects that are intended to increase the resilience of public and private infrastructure. Congressional action is needed to adopt the legislative proposal; once implemented, the proposal will require funding through appropriations to provide grants to projects and programs that address its intent.

Recommendation 3.2 – Develop and Maintain Continuity of the Economy Planning: The FY21 NDAA authorized the development of a Continuity of the Economy Plan (Section 9603), but the administration has not yet indicated which federal agency will lead this effort or what role the National Cyber Director will play in it. The legislation directs the President to coordinate with relevant federal agencies and the private sector in developing a plan for creating a Continuity of the Economy plan to provide for the restoration of the U.S. economy in the event of a significant drop in economic activity caused by a cyberattack or other serious event. The CSC's congressional Commissioners submitted a letter to the appropriations committees recommending that funds be appropriated to support a team at CISA to implement this planning requirement.

Recommendation 3.3 – Codify a "Cyber State of Distress" Tied to a "Cyber Response and Recovery Fund": This recommendation is a key priority for the CSC, and its implementation will require legislation to codify the process of declaring a "cyber state of distress" in the event of, or in preparation for, a significant cyber incident or series of incidents. Once that declaration is made, federal agencies can then scale up or augment the capabilities by drawing on an existing fund. The President's Budget Request included $20 million for the establishment of a Cyber Response and Recovery Fund.[51] In addition, the Senate-passed USICA legislation includes key provisions based on a bill introduced by Senators Gary Peters and Rob Portman that, if passed by the House, would fulfill the intent of this proposal.[52] Section 4252 authorizes the Secretary of Homeland Security, in consultation with the National Cyber Director, to make a declaration of a significant incident, after which the Director has the responsibility to coordinate asset response activities with other federal agencies, public and private entities,

---

49   National Risk Management Act of 2021, S. 1350, 117th Cong. (2021), https://www.congress.gov/bill/117th-congress/senate-bill/1350/.

50   USICA, §§ 4461–4462.

51   Shalanda D. Young, Acting Director Office of Management and Budget, letter to the Honorable Patrick Leahy, Chairman, Committee on Appropriations, United States Senate, April 9, 2021, with enclosure, "Summary of the President's Discretionary Funding Request," 16, https://www.whitehouse.gov/wp-content/uploads/2021/04/FY2022-Discretionary-Request.pdf, 16; U.S Department of Homeland Security, *Cybersecurity and Infrastructure Security Agency: Budget Overview, Fiscal Year 2022*, 8.

52   Cyber Response and Recovery Act of 2021, S. 1316, 117th Cong. (2021), https://www.congress.gov/bill/117th-congress/senate-bill/1316/text.

SLTT governments, law enforcement agencies, and emergency management and response agencies. The section also creates a Cyber Response and Recovery Fund for supporting asset-response activities and providing technical assistance following such a declaration.[53]

Recommendation 3.3.1 – Designate Responsibilities for Cybersecurity Services under the Defense Production Act: The Commission expected and has encountered significant pressure against this recommendation, which is one of the four that face known significant barriers to implementation.

Recommendation 3.3.2 – Clarify Liability for Federally Directed Mitigation, Response, and Recovery Efforts: This recommendation will require legislative action. In 2020 CSC staff drafted legislation to enable this proposal, which directs Congress to specify that any entities taking, or refraining from taking, action at the duly authorized direction of any agency head or any other federal official authorized by law will be insulated from legal liability.

Recommendation 3.3.3 – Improve and Expand Planning Capacity and Readiness for Cyber Incident Response and Recovery Efforts: This recommendation requires executive action, and CSC staff have proposed text for the needed executive order. Full implementation would include revising the National Cyber Incident Response Plan to add scenario-specific and sector-specific annexes drafted in consultation with sector-specific agencies and the Sector Coordinating Councils, accounting for options to mobilize additional resources to augment the government's response efforts, and integrating planning efforts with existing emergency response and disaster recovery programs operated by federal and SLTT entities. Section Six of the Biden administration's executive order on improving the nation's cybersecurity requires the development of a playbook that would drive planning to improve and standardize processes for federal cyber incident response.[54] This order does not precisely implement the CSC's recommendation, because the Commission focused on planning that involved a broader group of stakeholders rather than just the federal government. However, it has a similar intent as the Commission's recommendation and helps lay the groundwork for future progress.

Recommendation 3.3.4 – Expand Coordinated Cyber Exercises, Gaming, and Simulation: CSC congressional Commissioners recommended an increase in appropriations for FY21 to support this recommendation. The Consolidated Appropriations Act for FY21 allocated just under $22.8 million to the National Infrastructure Simulation Analysis Center, an amount that meets the requirements for this recommendation.[55]

Recommendation 3.3.5 – Establish a Biennial National Cyber Tabletop Exercise: Section 1744 of the FY21 NDAA accomplished this recommendation, and the CSC's congressional Commissioners submitted a letter to the appropriations committees recommending a small increase in funding to the CISA Exercises account in Infrastructure Assessments and Security in order to support development and execution of the exercise for FY22. The President's Budget Request for FY22 includes an increase to the CISA Exercises account of approximately $2 million and specifically addresses the exercise required by Section 1744.[56]

53   USICA, §§ 4251– 4252.

54   Exec. Order No. 14028.

55   U.S. Congress, Joint Explanatory Statement, Division F, 48.

56   United States Department of Homeland Security, *Cybersecurity and Infrastructure Security Agency: Budget Overview Fiscal Year 2022*, 253.

Recommendation 3.3.6 – Clarify the Cyber Capabilities and Strengthen the Interoperability of the National Guard: Section 1729 of the FY21 NDAA accomplished this recommendation, which appropriations will be needed to execute. The legislation directs the Secretary of Defense to evaluate the statutes, rules, regulations, and standards that pertain to the use of the National Guard for the response to and recovery from significant cyber incidents, and to issue updates to existing plans and policies as needed. At a hearing held by the House Armed Services Subcommittee on Cyber, Innovative Technologies, and Information Systems, Deputy Assistant Secretary of Defense for Cyber Policy Mieke Eoyang indicated that the Biden administration is undertaking the review required by the FY21 NDAA and expects to complete it during the summer.[57]

Recommendation 3.4 – Improve the Structure and Enhance Funding of the Election Assistance Commission: Legislation and appropriations are needed to accomplish this recommendation. H.R. 1, which was passed by the House of Representatives on March 3, 2021, includes a bipartisan amendment—co-sponsored by CSC Commissioners Representatives Jim Langevin and Mike Gallagher—on improving the Election Assistance Commission (EAC); it would clarify the duties of the EAC as they relate to the development and maintenance of cybersecurity guidelines and create the position of the Senior Cyber Policy Advisor to support the EAC's work.[58] In addition, in February 2021 the EAC voted to approve an updated version of the Voluntary Voting System Guidelines, which are used in the testing and certification of voting equipment.[59] The CSC's recommendation encouraged an updating of the guidelines, which were then more than six years old.[60] The Consolidated Appropriations Act for FY21 only partially addressed the CSC's request for an increase in appropriations. Accordingly, the CSC's congressional Commissioners submitted a letter to the appropriations committees recommending a further increase in appropriations for FY22 in support of this recommendation. The President's FY22 Budget Request includes an increase of approximately $5.8 million in funding for the EAC.[61]

Recommendation 3.4.1 – Modernize Campaign Regulations to Promote Cybersecurity: This recommendation requires legislative action. CSC staff have proposed legislation for this recommendation that amends the Federal Election Campaign Law to allow corporations to provide free and/or reduced-cost cybersecurity assistance to political campaigns on a nonpartisan basis.

Recommendation 3.5 – Build Societal Resilience to Foreign Malign Cyber-Enabled Information Operations: Legislation and appropriations are needed to accomplish this recommendation. To that end, CSC staff have put forward two legislative proposals. The first establishes a grant program for the development of education programs enabling Americans to identify foreign malign cyber-enabled information operations. The second commissions a GAO study on the effectiveness of existing cybersecurity education programs and establishes a grant program for research on the effectiveness of cybersecurity literacy curricula. In addition to a request in support of cybersecurity awareness at CISA, the CSC's congressional Commissioners submitted a letter to the appropriations committees recommending an increase in funding of $15 million for FY21 in support of relevant Department of Education programs, of which only $250,000 was appropriated, and made further recommendations in FY22 appropriations. The CSC's congressional Commissioners also recommended an increase in funding in support of a Department of Defense (DoD) pilot program on civics education created in Section 234 of the FY20

---

57   Eoyang, testimony at hearing, "Operations in Cyberspace and Building Cyber Capabilities Across the Department of Defense," at 36:59.

58   For the People Act of 2021, H.R. 1, § 3002(a),(g), 117th Cong. (2021), https://www.congress.gov/bill/117th-congress/house-bill/1/text.

59   Maggie Miller, "Election Commission Approves New Guidelines to Secure, Update Voting Equipment," *The Hill*, February 10, 2021, https://thehill.com/policy/cybersecurity/538216-election-commission-approves-new-guidelines-to-secure-update-voting.

60   "Voluntary Voting System Guidelines," U.S. Election Assistance Commission (2021), https://www.eac.gov/voting-equipment/voluntary-voting-system-guidelines.

61   U.S. Election Assistance Commission, "Fiscal Year 2022 Congressional Budget Justification" (2021), 16, https://www.eac.gov/sites/default/files/cbj/FY_2022_CBJ.pdf.

NDAA. The Consolidated Appropriations Act for FY21 included a more modest increase of $2 million for civics education. Accordingly, the CSC's congressional Commissioners recommended an additional increase in FY22, as well as additional funding in other departments to promote digital civics education, media literacy, and academic improvements in civics and history.

Recommendation 3.5.1 – Reform Online Political Advertising to Defend against Foreign Influence in Elections: This recommendation requires legislative action. CSC staff proposed such legislation, which is included among the drafts published in 2020; it calls for amending the Federal Election Campaign Act to specifically require that all U.S. online political advertisements be subject to the same restrictions on foreign national purchases as those in place for advertisement in traditional media.[62]

PILLAR FOUR: RESHAPE THE CYBER ECOSYSTEM TOWARD GREATER SECURITY

Assessment of Overall Pillar Progress

The past year saw partial implementation of recommendations that will be valuable in strengthening the cybersecurity ecosystem. The reporting requirements of Section 9005 of FY21 NDAA are early steps toward fully implementing the Commission's recommendations for research on insurance certification (Recommendation 4.4), while Section 9006 requires a strategy to implement Domain-based Message Authentication, Reporting, and Conformance (DMARC) across all U.S. email providers (addressing one of the three technological foundations that the Commission highlighted in Recommendation 4.5.2). Though very valuable, this progress is modest, and key priorities have yet to be achieved. Nevertheless, the Commission has made significant strides in terms of public engagement to gather input, refine, and build momentum around its priorities for 2021: setting up a National Cybersecurity Certification and Labeling Authority (Recommendation 4.1), establishing a Bureau of Cyber Statistics (Recommendation 4.3), amending Sarbanes-Oxley (Recommendation 4.4.4), and passing national data breach notification legislation (Recommendation 4.7.1). The Commission will also be prioritizing increased appropriations for NIST, an agency that plays an especially critical role in enabling stronger security across the national cyber ecosystem.

Rec. Number	Recommendation Title	Status	Assessment
4.1	Establish and Fund a National Cybersecurity Certification and Labeling Authority	Legislation Proposed, Related Executive Order Issued	
4.1.1	Create or Designate Critical Technology Security Centers	Appropriations Needed; Legislation Proposed	
4.1.2	Expand and Support the National Institute of Standards and Technology Security Work	Legislation Proposed; Significant Appropriations Needed	
4.2	Establish Liability for Final Goods Assemblers	Faces Significant Barriers to Implementation	
4.2.1	Incentivize Timely Patch Implementation	Appropriations Needed	

Table title: RESHAPE THE CYBER ECOSYSTEM TOWARD GREATER SECURITY

---

62 Montgomery, "Legislative Proposals."

4.3	Establish a Bureau of Cyber Statistics	Legislation Proposed	
4.4	Resource a Federally Funded Research and Development Center to Develop Cybersecurity Insurance Certifications	Partial Implementation via Legislation Passed in FY21 NDAA	
4.4.1	Establish a Public-Private Partnership on Modeling Cyber Risk	Executive Order Proposed	
4.4.2	Explore the Need for a Government Reinsurance Program to Cover Catastrophic Cyber Events	Executive Order Proposed; Partial Implementation via Legislation Passed in FY21 NDAA	
4.4.3	Incentivize Information Technology Security through Federal Acquisition Regulations and Federal Information Security Management Act Authorities	Implemented via Executive Order	
4.4.4	Amend the Sarbanes-Oxley Act to Include Cybersecurity Reporting Requirements	Legislation Proposed	
4.5	Develop a Cloud Security Certification	Executive or Legislative Action Needed, Legislation Proposed, Appropriations Needed, Related Executive Order Issued	
4.5.1	Incentivize the Uptake of Secure Cloud Services for Small and Medium-Sized Businesses and State, Local, Tribal, and Territorial Governments	Legislation Introduced, Appropriations Needed	
4.5.2	Develop a Strategy to Secure Foundational Internet Protocols and Email	Partial Implementation via Legislation Passed in FY21 NDAA, Further Implementation Possible via Executive Action or Legislation	
4.5.3	Strengthen the U.S. Government's Ability to Take Down Botnets	Legislation Introduced	
4.6	Develop and Implement an Information and Communications Technology Industrial Base Strategy	In Process via Executive Order	
4.6.1	Increase Support to Supply Chain Risk Management Efforts	Partial Implementation through Executive Order, Further Executive Action Needed	
4.6.2	Commit Significant and Consistent Funding toward Research and Development in Emerging Technologies	Partial Implementation through Legislation Passed by the Senate, Significant Appropriations Needed	
4.6.3	Strengthen the Capacity of the Committee on Foreign Investment in the United States	Appropriations Needed	
4.6.4	Invest in the National Cyber Moonshot Initiative	Appropriations Needed, Related Legislation Passed in FY21 NDAA	
4.7	Pass a National Data Security and Privacy Protection Law	Faces Significant Barriers to Implementation	
4.7.1	Pass a National Breach Notification Law	Legislation Proposed, Additional Legislation Proposed	

Recommendation Progress

Recommendation 4.1 – Establish and Fund a National Cybersecurity Certification and Labeling Authority: Authorizing legislation and appropriations are needed to accomplish this recommendation. However, progress can also be made through executive action, and the Biden administration's executive order on improving the nation's cybersecurity did help lay groundwork for future progress.[63] CSC staff also put forward a legislative proposal in support of this recommendation. If authorized, the National Cybersecurity Certification and Labeling Authority (NCCLA) will require the appropriation of funds. Absent such an authorization, the U.S. government can still make some, albeit limited, progress toward implementing this recommendation by appropriating funding for the Federal Communications Commission's Office of Engineering and Technology, Laboratory Division, to begin work to assess existing cybersecurity certifications pertinent to critical infrastructure and develop further resources as needed.

Recommendation 4.1.1 – Create or Designate Critical Technology Security Centers: A legislative change is needed to implement this recommendation; one approach is to amend the Homeland Security Act to specifically include critical technology security centers among the Homeland Security Advanced Research Projects Agency projects. Once authorized, the centers would need appropriated funding for this recommendation to be fully implemented.

Recommendation 4.1.2 – Expand and Support the National Institute of Standards and Technology Security Work: To address both the requirements of this recommendation and the related requirements in Recommendation 2.1.4 (see above), the CSC's congressional Commissioners submitted a letter to the appropriations committees recommending an increase in funding of $30 million for FY21 to support NIST's cybersecurity and privacy programs. The Consolidated Appropriations Act for FY21 did not include this increase, though the requirements for work on standards have grown rapidly. In particular, the recent executive order on improving the nation's cybersecurity requires the Director of NIST to establish best practices, guidelines, guidance, definitions, reviews, consultations, and other core elements needed to improve and standardize federal cybersecurity,[64] a tasking that makes this request even more urgent. Despite this expansion of its cybersecurity mission, the President's Budget Request recommended only a modest 6 percent increase to the Cybersecurity and Privacy budget function at NIST, while the agency-wide NIST budget grew almost 45 percent.[65] Recognizing NIST's critical role as an enabler of a stronger national cyber ecosystem nationwide, the CSC's congressional Commissioners recommended a much more significant increase to support NIST's cybersecurity and privacy programs for FY22.

Recommendation 4.2 – Establish Liability for Final Goods Assemblers: The Commission expected and has encountered significant pressure against this recommendation, which is one of the four that face known significant barriers to implementation. However, the recommendation has been drafted in proposed legislation and stands ready should a future emergency create the political impetus needed to overcome existing barriers.

Recommendation 4.2.1 – Incentivize Timely Patch Implementation: This recommendation can be implemented under existing authorities, but additional appropriations are required to support the development of a framework outlining patch implementation expectations and timelines. In a letter to congressional appropriators for FY22, the CSC's congressional Commissioners included a recommendation for report language to accompany the FY22 appropriations bill directing NIST

---

63 Exec. Order No. 14028.

64 Exec. Order No. 14028.

65 Mark Montgomery, "Biden's cyber budget good, but still insufficient to meet the threats." *The Hill*, June 15, 2021, https://thehill.com/opinion/cybersecurity/558507-bidens-cyber-budget-good-but-still-insufficient-to-meet-the-threats.

to detail its plans to update Special Publication 800-40, "Guide to Enterprise Patch Management Technologies," which was last revised in 2013.

Recommendation 4.3 – Establish a Bureau of Cyber Statistics: Authorizing legislation is needed to establish the bureau. The Commission staff proposed draft legislation during the 2020 legislative cycle, working with stakeholders and industry groups to clarify the relationship between the proposed bureau and the private sector. Following that process, CSC staff have proposed a revised draft for consideration during the 2021 legislative cycle. If authorized, the Bureau of Cyber Statistics will still require the appropriation of funds.

Recommendation 4.4 – Resource a Federally Funded Research and Development Center to Develop Cybersecurity Insurance Certifications: Section 9005 of the FY21 NDAA partially meets the intent of this recommendation by mandating a GAO study on the topic, but further executive action is required that will direct a federally funded research and development center to establish a training and certification program for underwriters and claims adjusters. CSC staff have provided text to the administration for an executive order in support of this recommendation.

Recommendation 4.4.1 – Establish a Public-Private Partnership on Modeling Cyber Risk: This recommendation requires executive action that will direct the U.S. government to conduct a study on the topic. CSC staff have provided text to the administration for a draft executive order that would establish a cross-sector working group, under the authority of CISA's Critical Infrastructure Partnership Advisory Council (CIPAC), focused on evaluating options for establishing a cyber incident data analysis repository and on assessing current laws, regulations, guidance, frameworks, and best practices concerning data collection and sharing and pricing cybersecurity risk. This working group would build off the initial work and findings of the Cyber Incident Data and Analysis Working Group, which also convened under the auspices of CIPAC during 2015 and 2016 and produced a number of key findings and conclusions that can inform the public-private partnership recommended by CSC.[66] While no new authorization is required, the CSC's congressional Commissioners recommended appropriations report language in support of the formation of this working group.

Recommendation 4.4.2 – Explore the Need for a Government Reinsurance Program to Cover Catastrophic Cyber Events: This recommendation was partially accomplished through Section 9005 of the FY21 NDAA, which mandated a GAO study on the cyber insurance industry. However, an executive order and some legislative action are required to direct the GAO, in consultation with the Department of Commerce, Department of Homeland Security (DHS), and Department of the Treasury, to conduct a study on the current state of the cyber insurance market, including the need for reinsurance.

Recommendation 4.4.3 – Incentivize Information Technology Security through Federal Acquisition Regulations and Federal Information Security Management Act Authorities: The CSC recommendation calls on the executive branch to direct the Federal Acquisition Regulation Council and OMB to update its cybersecurity regulations in the Federal Acquisition Regulations (FARs) and cybersecurity guidance under the Federal Information Security Management Act at least every five years. Executive Order 14028, "Improving the Nation's Cybersecurity," meets the intent of this recommendation. Sections Two and Four of the executive order lean heavily on federal acquisition to incentivize information technology (IT) security, explicitly referring to the FARs several times. The executive branch can help ensure the effectiveness of these changes by continuing to regularly update the regulations.

---

66   "Cybersecurity Insurance," Cybersecurity and Infrastructure Security Agency, accessed March 22, 2021, https://www.cisa.gov/cybersecurity-insurance.

Recommendation 4.4.4 – Amend the Sarbanes-Oxley Act to Include Cybersecurity Reporting Requirements: As an amendment to existing legislation, this recommendation can be accomplished only through legislative means. Legislation for this amendment proposed by Commission staff will clarify cybersecurity oversight and reporting requirements for publicly traded companies by amending the Sarbanes-Oxley Act to explicitly account for cybersecurity and require penetration testing of security systems.

Recommendation 4.5 – Develop a Cloud Security Certification: This recommendation can be accomplished through a combination of legislative and executive action and requires appropriations. Though not precisely meeting the intent of this recommendation, the Biden administration's executive order on improving the nation's cybersecurity does move the conversation on cloud security within the federal government forward by mandating updates to agency plans to secure cloud services as well as updates to guidance for the Federal Risk and Authorization Management Program (FedRAMP).[67] In addition, CSC staff have proposed legislation in support of this recommendation. While some elements of this recommendation require further authorization, support through appropriations can help advance the activities covered under existing authorities. Ideally, the cloud security certification would be established through NCCLA, which would coordinate with NIST to develop metrics and standards for a secure cloud benchmark and serve as the certifying agent responsible for conducting initial and subsequent audits of eligible applicants. But even without congressional authorization for NCCLA, work on the cloud security certification can still move forward through executive or legislative action directing DHS to spearhead the effort and serve as the certifying agent, in coordination with NIST. The draft legislation proposed by CSC staff on the topic includes language for both circumstances, ensuring that whether or not NCCLA exists, Congress has model text that can be used to establish a federal cloud security certification. The CSC's congressional Commissioners submitted a letter to the appropriations committees recommending increased appropriations for joint efforts at CISA and NIST to enable the research needed to build a foundation for a cloud security certification and to allow CISA to serve as the certifying agent if NCCLA is not authorized.

Recommendation 4.5.1 – Incentivize the Uptake of Secure Cloud Services for Small and Medium-Sized Businesses and State, Local, Tribal, and Territorial Governments: Legislation introduced in the 116th Congress—The State and Local IT Modernization and Cybersecurity Act[68]—addressed this recommendation and included a provision for the appropriation of funds, but it was not passed. In the coming months, the Commission expects to pursue legislation to implement this recommendation.

Recommendation 4.5.2 – Develop a Strategy to Secure Foundational Internet Protocols and Email: This recommendation was partially fulfilled through Section 9006 of the FY21 NDAA. That section deviates slightly from the intent of the legislation proposed by CSC staff in 2020 in that it calls only for the creation of a strategy to implement DMARC across all U.S. email providers, without addressing the Border Gateway Protocol and Domain Name System. The CSC draft legislation covers the full intent of the initial proposal, and the Commission expects to pursue the remaining elements in the coming months.

Recommendation 4.5.3 – Strengthen the U.S. Government's Ability to Take Down Botnets: The draft legislation proposed by CSC staff for this recommendation calls on Congress to enact Section Four of the International Cybercrime Prevention Act,[69] which was proposed in 2018. The legislation would provide courts with broader authority to address illegal botnets.

---

67 Exec. Order No. 14028.

68 State and Local IT Modernization and Cybersecurity Act, H.R. 8048, 116th Cong. (2020), https://www.congress.gov/bill/116th-congress/house-bill/8048.

69 International Cybercrime Prevention Act, S. 3288, 115th Cong. (2018), https://www.congress.gov/bill/115th-congress/senate-bill/3288/text.

In June 2021, a bipartisan group of Senators reintroduced the International Cybercrime Prevention Act, including a section dedicated to botnet remediation.[70]

Recommendation 4.6 – Develop and Implement an Information and Communications Technology Industrial Base Strategy: This recommendation is in progress as a result of the Biden-Harris administration's executive order on America's supply chains.[71] The executive order directs a 100-day review of U.S. supply chains in key areas, including semiconductor manufacturing and advanced packaging supply chains and critical and strategic mineral supplies. The order also mandates the assessment of sectoral supply chains and a general review and recommendations, including those directed at congressional or executive action to strengthen the integrity of American supply chains. Once the review is complete pursuant to the executive order, it should inform a broader supply chain strategy effort that directs national investment priorities for ICT industrial capacity and research and development while focusing on coordination with trusted partners and allies in this effort.

Recommendation 4.6.1 – Increase Support to Supply Chain Risk Management Efforts: The February 24, 2021, executive order on America's supply chains requires reports on topics including risks in the semiconductor manufacturing and advanced packaging supply chains, which partially implements this recommendation.[72] Further implementation will require executive action to identify ways to improve collaboration with the private sector in order to limit risk to supply chains and implement the findings of the reports generated by the new executive order.

Recommendation 4.6.2 – Commit Significant and Consistent Funding toward Research and Development in Emerging Technologies: Increased federal investment in early-stage research is critical if policymakers are to understand challenges related to emerging technologies, including artificial intelligence, quantum information science, and 5G wireless technology—topics on which many of CSC's recommendations focus. In a broad sense, the USICA bill addresses the core of this recommendation; but in this case, the key to successful implementation will be the appropriations that support that work. The CSC's congressional Commissioners submitted a letter to the appropriations committees recommending an increase to appropriations for the Department of Defense's Foundational Artificial Intelligence Science and Alternative Computing for both FY21 and FY22.

Recommendation 4.6.3 – Strengthen the Capacity of the Committee on Foreign Investment in the United States (CFIUS): The CSC's congressional Commissioners submitted a letter to the appropriations committees recommending $26.4 million in FY21 for the Federal Judicial Center's education and training program to support the education of bankruptcy judges on the CFIUS process. The CSC has once again advocated for this recommendation in a letter to the congressional appropriations committees for FY22.

Recommendation 4.6.4 – Invest in the National Cyber Moonshot Initiative: The Cyber Moonshot Initiative, created in 2018, is intended to "make the Internet safe and secure for the functioning of Government and critical services for the American

---

70 "Whitehouse, Graham, Blumenthal, Tillis Reintroduce Legislation to Fight Cybercrime," Office of Senator Sheldon Whitehouse, June 17, 2021, https://www.whitehouse.senate.gov/news/release/whitehouse-graham-blumenthal-tillis-reintroduce-legislation-to-fight-cybercrime-.

71 Exec. Order No. 14017.

72 Exec. Order No. 14017.

people by 2028."[73] The FY21 NDAA addressed some principles highlighted by the initiative, but work remains. CSC will continue to recommend further investment in the initiative.

Recommendation 4.7 – Pass a National Data Security and Privacy Protection Law: The Commission expected and has encountered significant pressure against this recommendation, which is one of the four that face known significant barriers to implementation. However, the recommendation has been drafted in proposed legislation and stands ready should a future emergency create the political impetus needed to overcome existing barriers.

Recommendation 4.7.1 – Pass a National Breach Notification Law: This recommendation requires legislative action. CSC staff have drafted a proposal that combines breach notification legislation with limited elements of incident reporting legislation. The draft proposal, as well as several other national data breach notification proposals, is under consideration in Congress, and they have a moderate likelihood of passing.

PILLAR FIVE: OPERATIONALIZE CYBERSECURITY COLLABORATION WITH THE PRIVATE SECTOR

Assessment of Overall Pillar Progress

In 2020, the Joint Cyber Planning Office (Recommendation 5.4) was established in Section 1715 of the FY21 NDAA, and establishment of the office was funded in the Consolidated Appropriations Act for FY21. At the same time, Section 1731 initiated planning for an Integrated Cyber Center (Recommendation 5.3). Progress on these two recommendations represents a significant step in advancing the objectives of Pillar Five. However, two of the central elements of Pillar Five—the codification of the concept of Systemically Important Critical Infrastructure (Recommendation 5.1) and the establishment and funding of a Joint Collaborative Environment (Recommendation 5.2)—have yet to be addressed, and both will be priorities for the Commission's legislative efforts in 2021.

OPERATIONALIZE CYBERSECURITY COLLABORATION WITH THE PRIVATE SECTOR			
Rec. Number	Recommendation Title	Status	Assessment
5.1	Codify the Concept of "Systemically Important Critical Infrastructure"	Legislation Proposed	
5.1.1	Review and Update Intelligence Authorities to Increase Intelligence Support to the Broader Private Sector	Legislation Proposed, Executive Order Proposed	
5.1.2	Strengthen and Codify Processes for Identifying Broader Private-Sector Cybersecurity Intelligence Needs and Priorities	Legislation Proposed, Executive Order Proposed	
5.1.3	Empower Departments and Agencies to Serve Administrative Subpoenas in Support of Threat and Asset Response Activities	Legislation Passed in FY21 NDAA	

73 National Security Telecommunications Advisory Committee (NSTAC), "NSTAC Report to the President on a Cybersecurity Moonshot" (November 14, 2018), ES-1, 5, https://www.cisa.gov/sites/default/files/publications/NSTAC_CyberMoonshotReport_508c.pdf.

5.2	Establish and Fund a Joint Collaborative Environment for Sharing and Fusing Threat Information	Legislation Proposed, Related Executive Order Issued	🟨
5.2.1	Expand and Standardize Voluntary Threat Detection Programs	Executive Order Proposed, Legislation Proposed, Related Executive Action	🟨
5.2.2	Pass a National Cyber Incident Reporting Law	Legislation Proposed, Related Executive Action	🟧
5.2.3	Amend the Pen Register Trap and Trace Statute to Enable Better Identification of Malicious Actors	Legislation Proposed	🟨
5.3	Strengthen an Integrated Cyber Center within CISA and Promote the Integration of Federal Cyber Centers	Legislation Passed in FY21 NDAA, Legislation and Appropriations May Be Required for FY23	🟩
5.4	Establish a Joint Cyber Planning Cell under the Cybersecurity and Infrastructure Security Agency	Legislation Passed in FY21 NDAA, Related Executive Order Issued, Appropriations Included for FY21, Further Appropriations Needed for FY22	🟩
5.4.1	Institutionalize Department of Defense Participation in Public-Private Cybersecurity Initiatives	Legislation Passed in FY21 NDAA, Legislation and Appropriations May Be Required for FY23	🟩
5.4.2	Expand Cyber Defense Collaboration with Information and Communications Technology Enablers	Executive Action Required	🟨

Recommendation Progress

Recommendation 5.1 – Codify the Concept of "Systemically Important Critical Infrastructure": This recommendation, which is fundamentally legislative in nature, is one of the Commission's priorities for implementation. After gathering input from government and industry groups in 2020 and the first half of 2021, the Commission expects to focus in the coming months on supporting a legislative proposal that would require the Secretary of Homeland Security to define a process for designating entities as Systemically Important Critical Infrastructure, with coordination from Sector Risk Management Agencies and relevant regulatory authorities. Entities so designated would be subject to higher security standards; they would also receive increased intelligence and protection to prevent disruption or compromise.

Recommendation 5.1.1 – Review and Update Intelligence Authorities to Increase Intelligence Support to the Broader Private Sector: This recommendation can be implemented through either legislative or executive action. CSC staff have proposed legislation that would direct the executive branch to conduct a six-month comprehensive review of intelligence policies, procedures, and resources to identify and address key limitations in the ability of the intelligence community to provide support to the private sector. Staff have also provided text to the administration for a draft executive order that would initiate a similar review, and the Commission expects to pursue these parallel tracks in the coming months.

Recommendation 5.1.2 – Strengthen and Codify Processes for Identifying Broader Private-Sector Cybersecurity Intelligence Needs and Priorities: Like Recommendation 5.1.1, this recommendation requires legislation or executive action. Legislative language proposed by the CSC staff directs the Director of National Intelligence to work with the CISA Director and SRMAs to establish a formal, recurring process for soliciting and compiling input from critical infrastructure sectors to inform national intelligence priorities. These inputs would help identify potential targets of nation-state cyber threats, gaps in critical infrastructure cybersecurity efforts, ways to refocus information collection and analysis in support of addressing those gaps, and means to assist SRMAs in identifying priorities and coordinating with the intelligence community. The draft legislation also requires the Director of National Intelligence and the CISA Director to submit an annual report to Congress assessing how such critical infrastructure inputs are shaping intelligence collection and evaluating efforts to share information with critical infrastructure owners and operators. In addition, CSC staff have drafted an executive order for the administration that directs the same set of actions.

Recommendation 5.1.3 – Empower Departments and Agencies to Serve Administrative Subpoenas in Support of Threat and Asset Response Activities: Section 1716 of the FY21 NDAA accomplished this recommendation by providing administrative subpoena authority to CISA for the purpose of identifying and notifying an entity that owns or operates a device or system related to critical infrastructure facing a specific security vulnerability. The provision outlines the limits on information obtainable through the subpoena process as well as liability protections, interagency coordination processes, the process for notifying identified entities, and a requirement to establish internal procedures for issuing subpoenas and handling information obtained through such subpoenas.

Recommendation 5.2 – Establish and Fund a Joint Collaborative Environment for Sharing and Fusing Threat Information: The House version of the FY21 NDAA included a provision that would have established the Joint Collaborative Environment (JCE).[74] In parallel, Senator Angus King introduced an amendment to include the JCE in the Senate version of the bill,[75] but the provision was ultimately dropped from the final FY21 NDAA. Section 1631 of the House version of the FY21 NDAA faced White House opposition, owing to concerns about sufficient protections for intelligence sources and methods.[76] The Commission supports the reintroduction of this legislative proposal in the 117th Congress. Notably, the May 12, 2021, executive order on improving the nation's cybersecurity sets in motion a process to facilitate better information sharing among departments and agencies.[77] Though it does not actually establish the JCE, the executive order may help lay the groundwork for its future creation.

Recommendation 5.2.1 – Expand and Standardize Voluntary Threat Detection Programs: Elements of this recommendation can be implemented through either executive action or legislation, and it is making progress toward implementation. As part of the 100-day plan to protect U.S. critical infrastructure announced on April 20, 2021, the executive branch worked with critical infrastructure owners and operators to modernize enhanced detection efforts.[78] Meanwhile, CSC staff have provided the administration with text for an executive order to standardize threat detection programs by establishing a formal process to solicit and compile input from critical infrastructure providers. In addition, the proposal drafted in 2021 by CSC staff outlining a Joint Collaborative Environment (Recommendation 5.2) includes a Cyber Threat Data Standards

---

74 National Defense Authorization Act for Fiscal Year 2021 (as engrossed in the House), H.R. 6395, § 1631, 116th Cong. (2020), https://www.congress.gov/bill/116th-congress/house-bill/6395/text/eh.

75 166 Cong. Rec. S3233 (daily ed. June 24, 2020) (S.Amdt. 1712 submitted by Sen. King), https://www.congress.gov/congressional-record/2020/06/24/senate-section/article/S3212-1.

76 Mariam Baksh, "White House Cites Intel Sharing Efforts in NDAA Veto Threat," Nextgov, July 21, 2020, https://www.nextgov.com/cybersecurity/2020/07/white-house-cites-intel-sharing-efforts-raising-veto-option-against-ndaa/167084/.

77 Exec. Order No. 14028.

78 "Statement by NSC Spokesperson Emily Horne on the Biden Administration's Efforts to Protect U.S. Critical Infrastructure," The White House, April 20, 2021, https://www.whitehouse.gov/briefing-room/statements-releases/2021/04/20/statement-by-nsc-spokesperson-emily-horne-on-the-biden-administrations-efforts-to-protect-u-s-critical-infrastructure/.

and Interoperability Council, which, if established, would help coordinate and harmonize voluntary network monitoring or threat detection programs for critical infrastructure. Not all elements of this recommendation would require new authorities, and Congress can support expanding voluntary threat detection programs through appropriations to the Threat Hunting and Capacity Building functions at CISA. The CSC's congressional Commissioners submitted a letter to the appropriations committees recommending increased support for voluntary threat detection programs in FY22.

Recommendation 5.2.2 – Pass a National Cyber Incident Reporting Law: The Commission expected significant pressure against this recommendation; however, a series of high-profile cybersecurity events, including the recent SolarWinds incident, may prove sufficient to create impetus for its implementation,[79] and a number of pending legislative drafts suggest that future progress is possible. It may also be possible to incorporate some elements of the CSC staff–drafted legislative proposal in a national data breach notification law, which the Commission expects to pursue in the coming months. Notably, the May 12, 2021, executive order on improving the nation's cybersecurity further increases the viability of implementation.[80] While it does not directly advance the implementation of this recommendation, which is intended as a broad-based national requirement, the executive order does implement changes for federal contractors. Moreover, the Cyber Safety Review Board established by the order will make information on incidents more readily available. Although progress on the implementation of CSC's recommendation remains limited, these changes may signal an increasingly receptive environment for its implementation in the future.

Recommendation 5.2.3 – Amend the Pen Register Trap and Trace (PRTT) Statute to Enable Better Identification of Malicious Actors: As an amendment to existing legislation, this recommendation can be accomplished only by Congress. CSC staff have proposed the relevant legislation,[81] which amends the PRTT Law to provide private-sector entities with a broader range of defensive techniques to aid in identifying malicious actors.

Recommendation 5.3 – Strengthen an Integrated Cyber Center (ICC) within CISA and Promote the Integration of Federal Cyber Centers: Section 1731 of the FY21 NDAA initiated implementation of this recommendation by requiring a report that charts a course for future coordination of federal cybersecurity centers within an ICC. While CISA is now investigating and will report to Congress on the path forward for the ICC, the CSC's congressional Commissioners submitted a letter to the appropriations committees recommending an increase in funding for CISA's Operational Planning and Coordination, Threat Hunting, and Vulnerability Management accounts to ensure continued support for the currently authorized activities that would be brought under the umbrella of the ICC.

Recommendation 5.4 – Establish a Joint Cyber Planning Cell under the Cybersecurity and Infrastructure Security Agency: Section 1715 of the FY21 NDAA established the Joint Cyber Planning Office (JCPO), in line with this recommendation. The JCPO will coordinate cybersecurity planning and readiness across the federal government and work with SLTT government and private-sector stakeholders to address cyber threats and develop plans for protection, detection, response, and recovery. In the FY21 omnibus appropriations bill, Congress appropriated $10,568,000 above CISA's FY21 cybersecurity request to establish the JCPO.[82] For FY22, the CSC's congressional Commissioners submitted a letter to the appropriations com-

---

79   "SolarWinds Fallout Sparks Calls for Mandatory Incident Reporting, Repercussions after Cyber Attacks," *Federal News Network*, February 24, 2021, https://federalnewsnetwork.com/cybersecurity/2021/02/solarwinds-fallout-sparks-calls-for-mandatory-incident-reporting-repercussions-after-cyber-attacks/.

80   Exec. Order. No. 14028.

81   CSC Staff, *Legislative Proposals*, 224.

82   U.S. Congress, Joint Explanatory Statement, Division F, 51.

RECOMMENDATIONS FROM THE CYBERSPACE SOLARIUM COMMISSION REPORT

mittees recommending an increase in appropriations to continue supporting the JCPO and providing it with the resources and personnel necessary to carry out its mission. The President's Budget Request includes an increase of $10 million for the JCPO in FY22.[83] Though not explicitly connected to the JCPO, the executive order on improving the nation's cybersecurity requires the development of playbooks for planning and conducting cybersecurity vulnerability and incident response activities.[84] These planning exercises may dovetail with the JCPO's intended purpose of working across the federal government as it develops plans.

Recommendation 5.4.1 – Institutionalize Department of Defense Participationin Public-Private Cybersecurity Initiatives: Section 1728 of the FY21 NDAA partly accomplished this recommendation by mandating that DoD undertake the review of public-private cybersecurity initiatives. Unlike the CSC proposal,[85] however, it does not require coordination with DHS. In the coming months, CSC expects that additional legislation and appropriations may be necessary in FY22 to implement the recommendations on institutionalizing and strengthening the initiatives reviewed pursuant to Section 1728.

Recommendation 5.4.2 – Expand Cyber Defense Collaboration with Information and Communications Technology Enablers: This recommendation requires executive action to direct the U.S. government to provide more and more actionable information to internet service providers, cloud service providers, information technology software and hardware producers, and cybersecurity companies and to collaborate on cyber defense efforts by building new institutional mechanisms and operationalizing existing public-private partnerships.

PILLAR SIX: PRESERVE AND EMPLOY THE MILITARY INSTRUMENT OF POWER

Assessment of Overall Pillar Progress

Of the pillars of the original Commission report, Pillar Six is among the closest to full implementation. The reason for this success is that the primary legislative vehicle for the Commission's recommendations in 2020 was the National Defense Authorization Act. Because of the pillar's topical focus on military issues, many of the recommendations it contained involved no congressional committees beyond the Senate Armed Services Committee and the House Armed Services Committee, which simplified the pathway to implementation for these legislative recommendations. Consequently, key Recommendations 6.1 and 6.2 were both fully implemented in the FY21 NDAA, and many other priorities were at least partially implemented. Notably, Section 1711 eliminates a spending cap on the Cyber Command operations procurement fund, which partially resolves the barrier identified in Recommendation 6.1.1. Further priorities remain for the Commission's work in 2021. In particular, significant elements of Recommendation 6.1.6, which calls for additional reporting metrics, have not yet been addressed. Developing such metrics will be crucial to evaluating the success of cyberspace policy and strategy going forward, and thus will be a focus of the Commission's legislative work in the coming months.

---

83   U.S. Department of Homeland Security, *Cybersecurity and Infrastructure Security Agency: Budget Overview Fiscal Year 2022*, 68.

84   Exec. Order No. 14028.

85   CSC Staff, *Legislative Proposals*, 232.

PRESERVE AND EMPLOY MILITARY INSTRUMENTS OF POWER			
Rec. Number	Recommendation Title	Status	Assessment
6.1	Direct the Department of Defense to Conduct a Force Structure Assessment of the Cyber Mission Force	Legislation Passed in FY21 NDAA	
6.1.1	Direct DoD to Create a Major Force Program Funding Category for U.S. Cyber Command	Partial Implementation via Legislation Passed in FY21 NDAA, Appropriations Needed	
6.1.2	Expand Current Malware Inoculation Initiatives	Executive Action Required	
6.1.3	Review Delegation of Authorities for Cyber Operations	Legislation Passed in FY21 NDAA	
6.1.4	Reassess and Amend Standing Rules of Engagement and Standing Rules for Use of Force for U.S. Forces	Executive Order Proposed	
6.1.5	Cooperate with Allies and Partners to Defend Forward	Executive Order Proposed	
6.1.6	Require the Department of Defense to Define Reporting Metrics	Legislation Required	
6.1.7	Assess the Establishment of a Military Cyber Reserve	Legislation Passed in FY21 NDAA	
6.1.8	Establish Title 10 Professors in Cyber Security and Information Operations	Executive Action or Legislation Required	
6.2	Conduct Cybersecurity Vulnerability Assessment of All Segments of the NC3 and NLCC Systems & Continually Assess Weapon Systems' Cyber Vulnerabilities	Legislation Passed in FY21 NDAA, Related Executive Order Issued	
6.2.1	Require DIB Participation in a Threat Intelligence Sharing Program	Partial Implementation via Legislation Passed in FY21 NDAA, Further Legislation Possible	
6.2.2	Require Threat Hunting on Defense Industrial Base Networks	Partial Implementation via Legislation Passed in FY21 NDAA, Further Legislation Possible	
6.2.3	Designate a Threat-Hunting Capability across the Department of Defense Information Network	Executive Action Required	
6.2.4	Assess and Address the Risk to National Security Systems Posed by Quantum Computing	Legislation Passed in FY21 NDAA	

Recommendation Progress

Recommendation 6.1 – Direct the Department of Defense to Conduct a Force Structure Assessment of the Cyber Mission Force (CMF): This recommendation was largely accomplished by Section 1706 of the FY21 NDAA, which mandates a comprehensive force structure assessment of the Cyber Operations Forces. The provision deviates slightly from the draft legislation proposed by CSC staff[86]—the force structure assessment of the CMF is contained under the broader umbrella of the Cyber Operations Forces—but this difference is minor, and the provision meets the intent of the CSC recommendation. General Paul Nakasone testified before the House Armed Services Subcommittee on Cyber, Innovative Technologies and Information Systems that an assessment that meets the intent of this recommendation is under way.[87]

Recommendation 6.1.1 – Direct DoD to Create a Major Force Program Funding Category for U.S. Cyber Command: Portions of the FY21 NDAA—Sections 1711 and 1746—partially meet the intent of this recommendation by, respectively, removing the $75 million cap on spending and requiring a report that contains recommendations on enabling the Commander of U.S. Cyber Command to execute budget and acquisition authorities in excess of imposed funding limits. However, the legislation does not create a Major Force Program funding category.

Recommendation 6.1.2 – Expand Current Malware Inoculation Initiatives: This recommendation requires executive action to accelerate the appropriate release of identified malicious code and other information gleaned from threat hunting and related activities that could aid defensive efforts. In releasing this information, the executive branch should also work to better coordinate the efforts of federal departments and agencies, the private sector, and allies and partners to improve the timing, granularity, and actionability of released malware samples. The U.S. government should pay specific attention to integrating the new enhanced coordination mechanisms proposed by other CSC recommendations and to releasing information to relevant private-sector stakeholders as quickly as is feasible.

Recommendation 6.1.3 – Review the Delegation of Authorities for Cyber Operations: Like Recommendation 6.1, this recommendation was authorized in FY21 NDAA Section 1706, which focuses on improving the quadrennial cyber posture review. Specifically, the provision calls for an "evaluation of the adequacy of mission authorities for all cyber-related military components, defense agencies, directorates, centers, and commands" and "assessment of the need for further delegation of cyber-related authorities, including those germane to information warfare, to the Commander of United States Cyber Command."[88]

Recommendation 6.1.4 – Reassess and Amend Standing Rules of Engagement (SROE) and Standing Rules for Use of Force (SRUF) for U.S. Forces: This recommendation will require executive action. CSC staff have drafted text for an executive order that requires a review of SROE/SRUF to ensure that they are relevant to action in and through cyberspace.

Recommendation 6.1.5 – Cooperate with Allies and Partners to Defend Forward: This recommendation will require executive action. CSC staff have drafted text for an executive order that mandates a review of the impact of defend forward and of persistent engagement on partners and allies, as well as an assessment of opportunities for collaboration and coordination with partners and allies in this area. Discussions with allies and partners, particularly those in NATO, during President Biden's June 2021 visit to Europe signal an intent to engage in these activities, an intent which is also reflected in the recent joint

---

86   CSC Staff, *Legislative Proposals*, 234.

87   Nakasone, testimony at hearing, "Operations in Cyberspace and Building Cyber Capabilities Across the Department of Defense," at 28:00.

88   FY21 NDAA, § 1706.

statement attributing malicious cyber activity and irresponsible state behavior to the government of China,[89] but implementation will require turning those discussions into action.

Recommendation 6.1.6 – Require the Department of Defense to Define Reporting Metrics: This recommendation requires executive action or additional legislation. Section 1634 of the FY20 NDAA requires DoD to conduct quarterly assessments of the readiness of the Cyber Mission Forces and establish metrics to inform such assessments.[90] Pursuant to Section 1634, the Secretary of Defense is required to submit quarterly briefings to the congressional defense committees on the department's progress in developing such metrics. CSC's recommendation instructs DoD to ensure that they go beyond readiness to also include measures of defend forward outcomes across strategic, operational, and tactical levels. Such metrics can be added to DoD's reporting requirements through either executive or legislative action, which should make clear how defend forward outcomes are to be measured.

Recommendation 6.1.7 – Assess the Establishment of a Military Cyber Reserve: This recommendation was authorized in FY21 NDAA Section 1730, which requires the Principal Cyber Advisor to the Secretary of Defense to submit to the congressional defense committees an assessment of reserve models tailored to support DoD's cyberspace operations.

Recommendation 6.1.8 – Establish Title 10 Professors in Cyber Security and Information Operations: This recommendation could be carried out through either legislation or executive action. In the coming months, the Commission plans to work with stakeholders in the executive branch to support the implementation of this recommendation, but notes that a legislative intervention—a revision to the Joint Professional Military Education standards and the designation of centers of excellence—would be longer lasting.

Recommendation 6.2 – Conduct Cybersecurity Assessment across the NC3 and NLCC Systems & DoD Vulnerability Assessment of Weapon Systems: This recommendation was authorized in FY21 NDAA Sections 1712 and 1747. Section 1712 mandates an evaluation of cyber vulnerabilities of major DoD weapons systems, the establishment of policies and requirements, and the identification of a senior official responsible for reassessments of major weapons systems. This mandate largely meets the intent of CSC's recommendation, though legislative language proposed by CSC staff called specifically for the assessment to include vulnerabilities across networked systems and the interaction of modern and legacy systems.[91] Section 1747 mandates the creation of a plan for acting on the findings and recommendations of the first annual assessment of cyber resiliency of nuclear command and control systems; it also requires the development of a concept of operations and oversight mechanism for cyber defense of such systems. The May 12, 2021, executive order on improving the nation's cybersecurity further advances the implementation of this recommendation by requiring the Secretary of Defense to issue a national security memorandum detailing cybersecurity practices for national security systems that meet or exceed the level of security outlined for federal civilian agencies in the executive order,[92] which this recommendation did not consider.

89   Maggie Miller, "NATO Members Agree to New Cyber Defense Policy," *The Hill*, June 14, 2021, https://thehill.com/policy/cybersecurity/558383-nato-member-states-agree-to-new-cyber-defense-policy-following; "The United States, Joined by Allies and Partners, Attributes Malicious Cyber Activity and Irresponsible State Behavior to the People's Republic of China," The White House, July 19, 2021, https://www.whitehouse.gov/briefing-room/statements-releases/2021/07/19/the-united-states-joined-by-allies-and-partners-attributes-malicious-cyber-activity-and-irresponsible-state-behavior-to-the-peoples-republic-of-china/.

90   National Defense Authorization Act for Fiscal Year 2020, Pub. L. No. 116-92, § 1634, 133 Stat. 1198 (2019), https://www.congress.gov/bill/116th-congress/senate-bill/1790/text.

91   CSC Staff, *Legislative Proposals*, 241.

92   Exec. Order No. 14028.

Recommendation 6.2.1 – Require Defense Industrial Base (DIB) Participation in a Threat Intelligence Sharing Program: This recommendation was partially authorized in Section 1737 of the FY21 NDAA, but that article does not fully meet the intent of the CSC recommendation. Rather than establishing a DIB threat intelligence program, the provision mandates a report from the Secretary of Defense on the feasibility and suitability of such a program. The bill does not require DoD to establish the program after the report is issued, instead leaving that decision to the discretion of the Secretary of Defense. It also characterizes the program as "threat information sharing" rather than "threat intelligence sharing." Additional legislation will be required to fulfill the intent of the initial proposal.

Recommendation 6.2.2 – Require Threat Hunting on Defense Industrial Base (DIB) Networks: This recommendation was partially authorized in Section 1739 of the FY21 NDAA, but that article does not fully meet the intent of the CSC recommendation. Section 1739 has much the same relation to this recommendation as to the previous recommendation: it calls for an assessment on the feasibility and suitability of a DIB threat-hunting program but does not require DoD to establish the program after the report is issued, instead leaving that decision to discretion of the Secretary of Defense. Additional legislation will be required to fulfill the intent of the initial proposal.

Recommendation 6.2.3 – Designate a Threat-Hunting Capability across the Department of Defense Information Network (DoDIN): This recommendation will require executive action. In June 2020, the Defense Information Systems Agency granted authority to ThreatQuotient to operate its ThreatQ offering on the DoDIN, which would enable threat hunting, among other functions.[93] No DoD force structure element has been established to perform this function, but if the threat-hunting capability exists, its implementation would likely meet the intent of the recommendation.

Recommendation 6.2.4 – Assess and Address the Risk to National Security Systems Posed by Quantum Computing: This recommendation was put into law in Section 1722 of the FY21 NDAA, which mandates a comprehensive assessment of current and potential risks to critical national security systems posed by quantum computing, with recommendations for research, development, and acquisition activities aimed at securing those critical national security systems from such risks and threats.

CYBERSPACE SOLARIUM COMMISSION WHITE PAPERS

To provide more detail on recommendations outlined in the U.S. Cyberspace Solarium Commission Report, the Commission produced a series of white papers in 2020. The first, published in May 2020, revisited the Commission's recommendations through the lens of the unfolding COVID-19 pandemic, examining both the manner in which the pandemic affected national cybersecurity and general lessons that could be drawn from managing a global crisis. The second white paper outlined in detail the Commission's vision for a National Cyber Director. Though it was drafted and shared with legislators in the spring of 2020, to provide room for deliberation first on draft legislation and then on policy implementation the paper has not yet been released publicly. The third and fourth white papers, published in autumn of 2020, focused on the federal cybersecurity workforce and the ICT supply chain, respectively; they articulated in separate recommendations many ideas that the original report had consolidated within single recommendations. Because their

---

93   Matthew Nelson, "DISA Approves ThreatQuotient Platform for DoD Information Network," ExecutiveBiz, June 11, 2020,
     https://blog.executivebiz.com/2020/06/disa-approves-threatquotient-platform-for-dod-information-network/.

publication was more recent, there has been less time to implement the more detailed actions outlined in the four white papers. Nevertheless, they are included in this assessment, and the Commission is pleased to report significant progress on many fronts.

WHITE PAPER #1: CYBERSECURITY LESSONS FROM THE PANDEMIC

Assessment of Overall White Paper Progress

Because the Commission's white papers were published after the original report, the timeline for implementing their recommendations has been shorter. However, this white paper has a notable exception: the recommendation to modernize state, local, tribal, and territorial information technology (Recommendation PAN1.1) is a direct outgrowth of the original report's Recommendation 4.5.1. This provision was the basis of the proposed State and Local IT Modernization and Cybersecurity Act in the 116th Congress,[94] which charts a course for the 117th Congress to follow in providing significant security improvements to state and local governments. Though the bill did not pass, it represents significant progress toward the recommendation's implementation and better cybersecurity, and this effort will continue to be a priority in 2021. Another key priority for the coming months will be the implementation of the Commission's recommendation to enhance assistance and recovery support for victims of cybercrime (Recommendation PAN1.3.b). Though not a new problem, fraud, abuse, and other internet-enabled crime have become especially pernicious during the COVID-19 pandemic, making passage of this legislation particularly timely: it will be a significant indicator of progress in this area in the coming months.

CYBERSECURITY LESSONS FROM THE PANDEMIC			
Rec. Number	Recommendation Title	Status	Assessment
PAN1.1	Provide State, Local, Tribal, and Territorial Government and Small and Medium-sized Business IT Modernization Grants	Legislation Proposed, Appropriations Needed	
PAN1.2	Pass an Internet of Things Security Law	Partial Implementation via Legislation Passed in FY21 NDAA, Related Executive Order Issued, Further Legislation Needed	
PAN1.3	Support Nonprofits That Assist Law Enforcement's Cybercrime and Victim Support Efforts	Legislation Proposed, Appropriations Needed	
PAN1.4	Increase Nongovernmental Capacity to Identify and Counter Foreign Disinformation and Influence Campaigns	Legislation Proposed, Appropriations Needed	
PAN1.4.1	Establish the Social Media Data and Threat Analysis Center	Authorized, Executive Action Required	

94   State and Local IT Modernization and Cybersecurity Act, H.R. 8048.

Recommendation Progress

PAN Recommendation 1.1 – Provide State, Local, Tribal, and Territorial Government and Small and Medium-sized Business IT Modernization Grants: CSC staff have proposed legislation for this recommendation, and it requires appropriations to be implemented. CSC Commissioners Representatives Langevin and Gallagher introduced the State and Local IT Modernization and Cybersecurity Act in the 116th Congress, which supported modernizing and securing state and local government information technology. The legislation did not pass; however, the CSC will be recommending its reintroduction in the 117th Congress.

PAN Recommendation 1.2 – Pass an Internet of Things Security Law: Section 9204 of the FY21 NDAA signaled Congress's increasing interest in the Internet of Things (IoT); it applies only to the federal government, however, not to the market as a whole. Meanwhile, the executive order on improving the nation's cybersecurity calls on the Director of NIST to identify IoT cybersecurity criteria for a consumer labeling program.[95] This does not implement the recommendation to create a national IoT security standard, but it does lay groundwork upon which a federal IoT security law may be built. Further legislation is needed to advance this recommendation, and the legislative language proposed by CSC staff for passing an IoT security law stresses the creation of enduring standards both for authentication and for patching.

PAN Recommendation 1.3 – Support Nonprofits That Assist Law Enforcement's Cybercrime and Victim Support Efforts: CSC staff have proposed legislation that would establish a federally supported nonprofit National Cybercrime Victim Assistance and Recovery Center to serve as a nationwide resource to provide information, technical assistance, and support to individuals and small businesses victimized by cybercrime. In 2020, CSC staff also proposed legislation supporting nonprofit organizations that work with law enforcement to provide victim assistance.

PAN Recommendation 1.4 – Increase Nongovernmental Capacity to Identify and Counter Foreign Disinformation and Influence Campaigns: CSC staff have proposed legislation that would authorize the Department of Justice, in consultation with the Department of Homeland Security, Department of State, and the National Science Foundation, to provide grants to nonprofit centers seeking to identify, expose, and explain malign foreign influence campaigns to the American public while putting those campaigns into context in order to avoid amplifying them. Appropriations will be needed to advance this recommendation, and the CSC's congressional Commissioners included a request in support of this recommendation in a letter to congressional appropriations committees for FY22.

PAN Recommendation 1.4.1 – Establish the Social Media Data and Threat Analysis Center: The center discussed in this recommendation was initially authorized by Section 5323 of the FY20 NDAA, which also specified that the effort may use up to $30 million of the funds appropriated to the National Intelligence Program for fiscal years 2020 and 2021. Section 9301 of the FY21 NDAA reaffirmed the requirement to establish a Social Media Data and Threat Analysis Center. The Social Media Data and Threat Analysis Center is long overdue. The Commission looks forward to seeing the law implemented with the establishment of the center. Meanwhile, the CSC's congressional Commissioners submitted a letter to the appropriations committees recommending continued appropriations through FY22 to support the effort.

---

95 Exec. Order No. 14028.

WHITE PAPER #2: NATIONAL CYBER DIRECTOR

NATIONAL CYBER DIRECTOR			
Rec. Number	Recommendation Title	Status	Assessment
NCD1	Establish a National Cyber Director	Legislation Passed in FY21 NDAA, Executive Action Under Way, Appropriations Needed	

Uniquely, this white paper has only one recommendation: establish a National Cyber Director. At the request of the Senate Armed Services Committee and the Senate Homeland Security and Governmental Affairs Committee in their letter dated May 14, 2020, the paper provides greater detail on Recommendation 1.3 from the original Cyberspace Solarium Commission Report. With the passage of Section 1752 of the FY21 NDAA, the actions outlined in this white paper have turned into a legal obligation that the President must implement. However, the Commission's job here is not done.

After a 60-day review of the position and its requirements,[96] the administration nominated Chris Inglis, who also served as a Commissioner with the Cyberspace Solarium Commission, for the role. The Senate held a confirmation hearing on June 10, 2021, and Chris Inglis was confirmed as the first National Cyber Director on June 17, 2021. On May 12, 2021, the Biden administration's executive order on improving the nation's cybersecurity further integrated the NCD into existing policy by clarifying that once the NCD is appointed, portions of the order may be updated to enable the NCD to execute their responsibilities.[97]

While the Biden-Harris administration has begun to adapt its National Security Council structures to include the NCD,[98] the relationship between the newly created position of Deputy National Security Advisor for Cyber and the NCD will have significant bearing on the NCD's overall authority. The FY21 NDAA designates the responsibilities and functions conferred to the NCD but in general assigns particular authorities with a light touch. Such authorities are ultimately derived from the President. As a consequence, the choices made by the Biden-Harris administration in defining the role of the National Cyber Director will largely dictate whether the NCD becomes a powerful tool for ensuring national cybersecurity or a mere technical requirement. One step Congress can take to ensure that the position is empowered to build a more secure cyberspace is to appropriate funding sufficient to enable adequate staffing, space, secure access to classified systems, and other necessities for the office's functionality. To that end, the CSC's congressional Commissioners submitted a letter to the appropriations committees including both a recommended funding amount and suggested language for the bill appropriating that funding. The President's FY22 Budget Request included $15 million for the establishment of the Office of the National Cyber Director.[99]

96 Ellen Nakashima, "Tension Grows between Congress and the Administration over How White House Cyber Policy Should Be Run," *Washington Post*, February 18, 2021, https://www.washingtonpost.com/national-security/biden-cybersecurity-policy-congress-tension/2021/02/18/7f9d7398-6c9b-11eb-ba56-d7e2c8defa31_story.html.

97 Exec. Order No. 14028.

98 Joseph R. Biden, Jr., "Memorandum Renewing the National Security Council System," February 4, 2021, https://www.whitehouse.gov/briefing-room/statements-releases/2021/02/04/memorandum-renewing-the-national-security-council-system/.

99 Office of Management and Budget, *Budget of the U.S. Government: Fiscal Year 2022*, 32.

Although this report considers Recommendation 1.3—and thus the recommendation of this white paper—technically implemented as a function of the passage of the FY21 NDAA, the Commission recognizes that a number of criteria must be met for the recommendation to be successful. In order to make meaningful improvements, the National Cyber Director must bring direction and coherence to national cybersecurity strategy, policy, and operations. The recommendation will be deemed successful when the position of the National Cyber Director brings leadership, coordination, and consistent advocacy for cybersecurity priorities within the White House.

WHITE PAPER #3: GROWING A STRONGER FEDERAL CYBER WORKFORCE

Assessment of Overall White Paper Progress

Many of the main barriers to progress outlined in the Commission's white paper on the federal cybersecurity workforce result from a lack of strategy, leadership, and coordination. If the position is established effectively, the National Cyber Director would bring these much-needed elements to developing the federal cybersecurity workforce. While the passage of Sections 9401 to 9407 of the FY21 NDAA made significant progress in implementing Recommendation 1.5 from the original Solarium report of 2020, an effective National Cyber Director could take major strides toward implementing Federal Cyber Workforce White Paper Recommendation 1 by creating the leadership and coordination structures, some of which would be led by the NCD, that would enable the white paper's other recommendations. Consequently, in the coming months the Commission expects to see significant progress on the executive-led recommendations from this white paper.

GROWING A STRONGER FEDERAL CYBER WORKFORCE			
Rec. Number	Recommendation Title	Status	Assessment
WF1	Establish Leadership and Coordination Structures	Executive Order Proposed	
WF2	Properly Identify and Utilize Cyber-Specific Occupational Classifications	Executive Order Proposed	
WF3	Develop Apprenticeships	Legislation Introduced, Executive Order Proposed	
WF4	Improve Cybersecurity for K-12 Schools	Legislation Proposed	
WF5	Provide Work-Based Learning via Volunteer Clinics	Executive Order Proposed	
WF6	Improve Pay Flexibility/Hiring Authority	Executive Order Proposed	
WF7	Incentivize Cyber Workforce Research	Legislation Proposed, Executive Order Proposed	
WF8	Mitigate Retention Barriers and Invest in Diversity, Equity, and Inclusion in Recruiting	Legislation Proposed, Executive Order Proposed	

Recommendation Progress

Federal Cyber Workforce White Paper Recommendation 1 – Establish Leadership and Coordination Structures: Executive action is required to implement this recommendation and establish the leadership and coordination structures necessary for strengthening the federal cyber workforce. CSC staff have provided text to the administration for an executive order that both would designate the Office of the National Cyber Director as the convener of an interagency working group tasked with overseeing the federal government's strategy for the cyber workforce and would create a separate interagency working group to support federal departments and agencies in implementing their agency-specific programs aimed at strengthening the cyber workforce.

Federal Cyber Workforce White Paper Recommendation 2 – Properly Identify and Utilize Cyber-Specific Occupational Classifications: Executive action is required to implement this recommendation. CSC staff have provided the administration with text for an executive order in support of this recommendation, which would commission a study that, in part, examines the viability of creating a cyber-specific occupational classification and considers potential congressional action needed for its creation.

Federal Cyber Workforce White Paper Recommendation 3 – Develop Apprenticeships: This recommendation requires congressional or executive action to establish a pilot apprenticeship program within CISA. Such a program would serve as a proof of concept for other federal departments and agencies, as well as SLTT governments seeking to establish registered apprenticeship programs. CSC supports the Federal Cybersecurity Workforce Expansion Act, introduced by Senators Maggie Hassan and John Cornyn in June 2021, which would implement this recommendation.[100]

Federal Cyber Workforce White Paper Recommendation 4 – Improve Cybersecurity for K-12 Schools: This recommendation requires congressional action for its implementation. In 2021, a bipartisan group of Representatives introduced the Enhancing K-12 Cybersecurity Act of 2021,[101] which CSC supports as a key means of implementing this recommendation. The legislation would create an information exchange, registry of cyber incidents, and a Technology Improvement Program for K-12 schools. A similar Senate bill, the K-12 Cybersecurity Act of 2021, works toward the same goal of securing K-12 schools by commissioning a study that will inform recommendations and an online training toolkit for K-12 officials.

Federal Cyber Workforce White Paper Recommendation 5 – Provide Work-Based Learning via Volunteer Clinics: Executive action is needed to implement this recommendation. CSC staff have provided the administration with a draft executive order that would create a grant program, overseen by the Office of the National Cyber Director, for institutions of higher education seeking to provide work-based learning opportunities via volunteer clinics that provide free cybersecurity services and training to individuals, nonprofit organizations, and small businesses in the grantee's community.

Federal Cyber Workforce White Paper Recommendation 6 – Improve Pay Flexibility/Hiring Authority: Executive action is needed to implement this recommendation. An executive order on federal cyber workforce coordination, drafted by CSC staff and provided to the administration, commissions a study to review existing pay flexibilities and hiring authorities that could strengthen the federal cyber workforce and recommend further action that would create additional flexibilities or authorities in support of the effective recruitment, development, and retention of the federal cyber workforce.

Federal Cyber Workforce White Paper Recommendation 7 – Incentivize Cyber Workforce Research: A bill passed by the House, the National Science Foundation for the Future Act, includes a cybersecurity workforce data initiative that would fulfill significant elements of this recommendation if it becomes law. Additionally, the CSC's congressional Commissioners submitted a letter to the appropriations committees recommending the funding of additional personnel to support the National Center for Science and Engineering Statistics in its efforts to identify, compile, and analyze existing nationwide data and

---

100 "Senators Hassan, Cornyn Introduce Bipartisan Bill to Strengthen Federal Cyber Workforce," Office of Senator Maggie Hassan, June 25, 2021, https://www.hassan.senate.gov/news/press-releases/senators-hassan-cornyn-introduce-bipartisan-bill-to-strengthen-federal-cyber-workforce.

101 Enhancing K-12 Cybersecurity Act, H.R. 4005, 117th Cong. (2021), https://www.congress.gov/bill/117th-congress/house-bill/4005/text.

conduct surveys as necessary to better understand the national cyber workforce. The CSC's congressional Commissioners also recommended increased funding for NIST's National Initiative for Cybersecurity Education to support regional programs as required by FY21 NDAA Section 9401. A proposed executive order drafted by CSC staff also details the creation of a grant program to incentivize research on the workforce, pathways to entry into the federal cyber workforce, and strategies for promoting diversity, equity, and inclusion in the federal cyber workforce.

Federal Cyber Workforce White Paper Recommendation 8 – Mitigate Retention Barriers and Invest in Diversity, Equity, and Inclusion in Recruiting: Congressional or executive action is needed to implement this recommendation. CSC staff have proposed draft legislative and executive order language in support of this recommendation, which would establish training programs for managers to cultivate practices that foster a more inclusive work environment, institutionalize a cyber career pathways program, and ask each cybersecurity agency to update its department- and agency-specific Diversity and Inclusion Strategic Plans, among other provisions. While not specific to cybersecurity, the Biden administration's June 25, 2021 Executive Order on Diversity, Equity, Inclusion, and Accessibility in the Federal Workforce takes steps towards prioritizing government-wide efforts to recruit, hire, and retain a more diverse and inclusive workforce.

WHITE PAPER #4: BUILDING A TRUSTED ICT SUPPLY CHAIN

Assessment of Overall White Paper Progress

Although "Building a Trusted ICT Supply Chain" was the most recently published of the white papers, its recommendations have also seen the most success in implementation (the single-recommendation white paper on the NCD aside). This progress is largely due to the Biden-Harris Administration's executive order on America's supply chains.[102] The reports mandated in this executive order put three recommendations of this white paper in process (SC1, SC2, and SC4), and helped create momentum in support of several others. Building on this momentum, the Commission expects in the coming months to prioritize two major legislative actions from this white paper: the establishment of a National Security Investment Corporation (SC3.3) and of a National Supply Chain Intelligence Center (SC4.1), which would create critical tools for constructing a trusted ICT supply chain.

BUILDING A TRUSTED ICT SUPPLY CHAIN			
Rec. Number	Recommendation Title	Status	Assessment
SC1	Develop and Implement an Information and Communication Technologies Industrial Base Strategy	In Process via Executive Order	
SC2	Identify Key Information and Communication Technologies and Materials	In Process via Executive Order	
SC3	Conduct a Study on the Viability of and Designate Critical Technology Clusters	Legislation Has Passed in the Senate	
SC3.1	Provide Research and Development Funding for Critical Technologies	Appropriations Needed, Executive Order Proposed	

102 Exec. Order No. 14017.

SC3.2	Incentivize the Movement of Critical Chip and Technology Manufacturing out of China	Legislation Proposed, Appropriations Needed	
SC3.3	Conduct a Study on a National Security Investment Corporation	Legislation Proposed, Proposed Executive Order	
SC4	Designate Lead Agency for ICT Supply Chain Risk Management	In Process via Executive Order	
SC4.1	Establish a National Supply Chain Intelligence Center	Legislation Proposed	
SC4.2	Fund Critical Technology Security Centers	Legislation Proposed, Appropriations Needed	
SC5	Incentivize Open and Interoperable Standards and Release More Mid-band Spectrum	Executive Action Needed, Executive Order Proposed	
SC5.1	Develop a Digital Risk Impact Assessment for International Partners for Telecommunications Infrastructure Projects	Legislation Proposed, Appropriations Needed, Executive Order Proposed	
SC5.2	Ensure That the EXIM, DFC, and USTDA Can Compete with Chinese State-owned and State-backed Enterprises	Legislation Proposed, Executive Order Proposed	
SC5.3	Develop a List of Contractors and Vendors Prohibited from Implementing Development Projects	Executive Order Proposed, Legislation Proposed	

Recommendation Progress

ICT Supply Chain White Paper Recommendation 1 – Develop and Implement an Information and Communication Technologies Industrial Base Strategy: This recommendation is in progress as a result of the Biden-Harris administration's executive order on America's supply chains. The executive order directs a 100-day review of U.S. supply chains in key areas, including semiconductor manufacturing, advanced packaging, and critical and strategic mineral supplies. The order also mandates the assessment of sectoral supply chains and a general review and recommendations, including those for congressional or executive action, to strengthen the integrity of American supply chains. Once the initial review is complete and, pursuant to the executive order, a process for quadrennial supply chain reviews has been established, the Biden-Harris administration should act on the findings and associated recommendations and publish an annually updated national supply chain strategy outlining the federal government's role in and means of securing the U.S. industrial base supply chain.

ICT Supply Chain White Paper Recommendation 2 – Identify Key Information and Communication Technologies and Materials: This recommendation is in progress as a result of the Biden-Harris administration's executive order on America's supply chains. The executive order directs an assessment of sectoral supply chains, including that of the ICT industrial base, to review the critical goods and materials supporting each supply chain.[103]

103 Exec. Order No. 14017.

ICT Supply Chain White Paper Recommendation 3 – Conduct a Study on the Viability of and Designate Critical Technology Clusters: This recommendation requires congressional action, and CSC staff have drafted legislation in support of the designation of American localities as critical technology clusters. CSC staff have also provided the administration with language for an executive order that commissions a study on the viability of such a strategy for stimulating domestic manufacturing. The Senate-passed USICA would create a regional technology hubs program that would meet the intent of this recommendation by providing strategy development and strategy implementation grants to support geographically based multi-stakeholder consortia focused on U.S. leadership in technology and innovation, regional economic development, the diffusion of innovation, and domestic job creation.[104] The FY21 NDAA included a number of provisions that aim to support domestic semiconductor and microelectronic manufacturing through a financial assistance program, a public-private partnership, a common funding mechanism for partner and allied supply chains, and research and development centers.[105] Though not organized around regional hubs, these actions promote the goal of strengthening the domestic production of critical technologies; USICA includes a provision that would authorize appropriations in support of several of these initiatives.[106]

ICT Supply Chain White Paper Recommendation 3.1 – Provide Research and Development Funding for Critical Technologies: In a broad sense, the USICA bill addresses some elements of this recommendation, but its successful implementation in this case will depend on the appropriations that support its work. The CSC's congressional Commissioners submitted a letter to the appropriations committees for FY22 recommending an increase in appropriations in support of this recommendation. CSC staff has provided the administration with a draft executive order that includes reviewing federal investment in research and development in emerging technologies; tasking the Office of Science and Technology Policy (OSTP) with coordinating with other relevant federal stakeholders to assess federal priorities, including OSTP budgetary priorities; and identifying opportunities to make progress in areas relevant to ICT supply chain security.

ICT Supply Chain White Paper Recommendation 3.2 – Incentivize the Movement of Critical Chip and Technology Manufacturing out of China: Congressional action is needed in order to implement this recommendation. CSC staff have proposed draft legislation that includes creating a dedicated fund for a grant program to provide incentives to companies for projects that move chip and technology manufacturing into the United States. Elements of the USICA bill do work toward a similar goal. For example, Section 3101 of the bill would authorize contracts with qualified experts to assist with supply chain management issues related to China, including exiting Chinese markets or relocating facilities. In the aggregate, however, the bill largely pursues different means than those outlined in the CSC recommendation, which calls on the U.S. government to work with companies to defray the cost of relocating manufacturing facilities.

ICT Supply Chain White Paper Recommendation 3.3 – Conduct a Study on a National Security Investment Corporation: Congressional action is needed to establish a public-private national security investment corporation that would coordinate investment in strategically important areas. CSC staff have proposed draft legislation and have provided the administration with text for an executive order commissioning a study on the viability of such a public-private corporation. Because this is one of its key priorities for the upcoming fiscal year, the CSC is engaging with relevant stakeholders and legislators to establish support for this recommendation.

---

104 USICA, § 2401.
105 FY21 NDAA, §§ 9902–9903, 9905–9906.
106 USICA, § 1002.

ICT Supply Chain White Paper Recommendation 4 – Designate Lead Agency for ICT Supply Chain: The Biden-Harris administration's executive order on America's supply chains represents an important first step in fulfilling this recommendation.[107] The executive order designates the Departments of Commerce and Homeland Security as responsible for carrying out the portions of the executive order related to the ICT industrial base, but further action can be taken to formally designate the Department of Commerce as the lead federal agency for ICT supply chain management after the review required by the executive order is completed.

ICT Supply Chain White Paper Recommendation 4.1 – Establish a National Supply Chain Intelligence Center: Congressional action is required to establish a National Supply Chain Intelligence Center, and CSC staff have provided draft legislation. The legislation would mandate an assessment of the viability of a national supply chain intelligence center focused on consolidating and coordinating federal supply chain intelligence efforts and coordinating with industry stakeholders.

ICT Supply Chain White Paper Recommendation 4.2 – Fund Critical Technology Security Centers: Congressional action and appropriations are needed to accomplish this recommendation, which mirrors Recommendation 4.1.1. CSC staff have developed a legislative proposal that would codify the existence of the centers.

ICT Supply Chain White Paper Recommendation 5 – Incentivize Open and Interoperable Standards and Release More Mid-band Spectrum: This recommendation requires executive action. CSC staff have provided the administration with language for an executive order that would facilitate the creation of a National 5G Deployment Plan, which would focus in part on options for reallocating mid-band spectrum for expanded 5G deployment.

ICT Supply Chain White Paper Recommendation 5.1 – Develop a Digital Risk Impact Assessment for International Partners for Telecom Infrastructure Projects: Congressional action and appropriations are needed to support this recommendation. The CSC's congressional Commissioners submitted a letter to the appropriations committees in support of the elements of this recommendation that can be done under existing authorities. To further advance the proposal, CSC staff have provided draft legislation to Congress that would direct the United States Agency for International Development (USAID) to work with international partners in developing a digital risk impact assessment that highlights the risks associated with the use of untrusted technologies in implementing digitization and telecommunications infrastructure projects.

ICT Supply Chain White Paper Recommendation 5.2 – Ensure That the Export-Import Bank (EXIM), U.S. International Development Finance Corporation (DFC), and United States Trade Development Agency (USTDA) Can Compete with Chinese State-owned and State-backed Enterprises: This recommendation requires congressional action, and CSC staff have provided draft legislation to Congress. CSC staff have also provided the administration with a draft executive order that would task relevant agencies with reviewing existing authorities, regulations, and legislation and recommending potential action to be taken in support of this recommendation.

ICT Supply Chain White Paper Recommendation 5.3 – Develop a List of Contractors and Vendors Prohibited from Implementing Development Projects: This recommendation requires executive action, and CSC staff have provided the administration with language for an executive order that calls on relevant departments and agencies to create a list of companies whose products cannot be used in federally funded development projects. CSC staff have provided draft legislation to Congress that would direct the executive branch to initiate the creation of such a list of prohibited vendors.

---

107 Exec. Order No. 14017.

ABBREVIATIONS

ALAT	Assistant Legal Attaché
CETAP	Cybersecurity Education and Training Assistance Program
CFIUS	Committee on Foreign Investment in the United States
CIPAC	Critical Infrastructure Partnership Advisory Council
CISA	Cybersecurity and Infrastructure Security Agency
CMF	Cyber Mission Force
CSC	U.S. Cyberspace Solarium Commission
CTIIC	Cyber Threat Intelligence Integration Center
DFC	U.S. International Development Finance Corporation
DHS	Department of Homeland Security
DIB	Defense Industrial Base
DMARC	Domain-based Message Authentication, Reporting, and Conformance
DoD	Department of Defense
DoDIN	Department of Defense Information Network
EAC	Election Assistance Commission
EDR	endpoint detection and response
EXIM	Export-Import Bank
FAR	Federal Acquisition Regulation
FedRAMP	Federal Risk and Authorization Management Program
FY	fiscal year
GAO	Government Accountability Office
ICC	Integrated Cyber Center
ICT	information and communications technology
IoT	Internet of Things
IT	information technology
JCE	Joint Collaborative Environment
JCPO	Joint Cyber Planning Office
MFP	Major Force Program
NC3	nuclear command, control, and communications

NCCLA	National Cybersecurity Certification and Labeling Authority
NCD	National Cyber Director
NDAA	National Defense Authorization Act
NIST	National Institute of Standards and Technology
NLCC	National Leadership Command Capabilities
NSF	National Science Foundation
NSTAC	National Security Telecommunications Advisory Committee
OCCIP	Office of Cybersecurity and Critical Infrastructure Protection
OSTP	Office of Science and Technology Policy
PRTT	Pen Register Trap and Trace
SLTT	state, local, tribal, and territorial
SRMA	Sector Risk Management Agency
SROE	Standing Rules of Engagement
SRUF	Standing Rules for Use of Force
SSA	sector-specific agencies
USAID	United States Agency for International Development
USICA	United States Innovation and Competition Act of 2021
USTDA	United States Trade Development Agency

COMMISSIONERS

STAFF